Contents

Project Management Institute

The Standard for Program Management

The Standard for Program Management
ISBN 13: 978-1-930699-54-0
ISBN 10: 1-930699-54-9

–Published by: Project Management Institute, Inc.
　　　　　　　Four Campus Boulevard
　　　　　　　Newtown Square, Pennsylvania 19073-3299 USA.
　　　　　　　Phone: +610-356-4600
　　　　　　　Fax: +610-356-4647
　　　　　　　E-mail: customercare@pmi.org
　　　　　　　Internet: www.pmi.org

PMI Publications welcomes corrections and comments on its books. Please feel free to send comments on typographical, formatting, or other errors. Simply make a copy of the relevant page of the book, mark the error, and send it to: Book Editor, PMI Publications, Four Campus Boulevard, Newtown Square, PA 19073-3299 USA, or e-mail: booked@pmi.org.

PMI books are available at special quantity discounts to use as premiums and sales promotions, or for use in corporate training programs, as well as other educational programs. For more information, please write to Bookstore Administrator, PMI Publications, Four Campus Boulevard, Newtown Square, PA 19073-3299 USA, or e-mail: booksonline@pmi.org. Or contact your local bookstore.

The paper used in this book complies with the Permanent Paper Standard issued by the National Information Standards Organization (Z39.48—1984).

10　9　8　7　6　5　4　3

Notice

The Project Management Institute, Inc. (PMI) standards and guideline publications, of which the document contained herein is one, are developed through a voluntary consensus standards development process. This process brings together volunteers and/or seeks out the views of persons who have an interest in the topic covered by this publication. While PMI administers the process and establishes rules to promote fairness in the development of consensus, it does not write the document and it does not independently test, evaluate, or verify the accuracy or completeness of any information or the soundness of any judgments contained in its standards and guideline publications.

PMI disclaims liability for any personal injury, property or other damages of any nature whatsoever, whether special, indirect, consequential or compensatory, directly or indirectly resulting from the publication, use of application, or reliance on this document. PMI disclaims and makes no guaranty or warranty, expressed or implied, as to the accuracy or completeness of any information published herein, and disclaims and makes no warranty that the information in this document will fulfill any of your particular purposes or needs. PMI does not undertake to guarantee the performance of any individual manufacturer or seller's products or services by virtue of this standard or guide.

In publishing and making this document available, PMI is not undertaking to render professional or other services for or on behalf of any person or entity, nor is PMI undertaking to perform any duty owed by any person or entity to someone else. Anyone using this document should rely on his or her own independent judgment or, as appropriate, seek the advice of a competent professional in determining the exercise of reasonable care in any given circumstances. Information and other standards on the topic covered by this publication may be available from other sources, which the user may wish to consult for additional views or information not covered by this publication.

PMI has no power, nor does it undertake to police or enforce compliance with the contents of this document. PMI does not certify, tests, or inspect products, designs, or installations for safety or health purposes. Any certification or other statement of compliance with any health or safety-related information in this document shall not be attributable to PMI and is solely the responsibility of the certifier or maker of the statement.

List of Figures and Tables

Foreword

On behalf of the Project Management Institute (PMI®) Board of Directors, I am pleased to present *The Standard for Program Management*.

Project management is one of those terms with multiple meanings. For a long time it was associated only with projects, but some twenty years ago that began to change, and today it is understood to include portfolio management and program management as well.

Today the *PMBOK® Guide* continues to be the *de facto* global standard for the project management of single projects, as well as an American National Standard. *The Standard for Program Management* describes a documented set of processes that represent generally recognized good practices in the discipline of program management. This significant new standard will do for programs and those working on programs what the *PMBOK® Guide* has done for projects.

I would like to sincerely thank the globally diverse project team that worked so diligently to bring this standard to fruition. The team, which consisted of a group of 416 PMI volunteers representing 36 countries, was led by project manager David W. Ross, PMP, and assisted by deputy project manager Paul E. Shaltry, PMP. Dedicated and competent volunteers have always been the backbone of PMI's success, and this publication is yet another example.

I trust that each of you will find this latest standard from PMI beneficial to yourself as well as to your organization.

Iain Fraser, Fellow PMINZ, PMP
2006 Chair—PMI Board of Directors

Preface

The Standard for Program Management will provide program managers the same wealth of information that is available to project managers in "The Standard for Project Management" in *A Guide to the Project Management Body of Knowledge (PMBOK® Guide)*. The target audience for this standard includes: senior executives, portfolio managers, program managers, project managers and their team members, members of a project or program management office, managers of program managers and project managers, customers and other stakeholders, educators, consultants, trainers and researchers. The standard builds on work postulated in the *Organizational Project Management Maturity Model (OPM3®)*.

The processes documented within this standard are generally recognized good practices and the necessary steps to successfully manage a program, and includes practices and skills such as:

- Benefits management, stakeholder management, program governance, and how these three themes are indispensable to successful program management.
- How program management can be used in organizational planning to ensure that all programs and projects are aligned with organizational objectives, efficiently coordinate work effort, and provide for the best use of resources within the programs.

Introduced to provide program managers with a resource to help them achieve organizational goals, *The Standard for Program Management* aims to provide a detailed understanding of program management and promote efficient and effective communication and coordination among various groups. With its ability to help assess the variety of factors linking projects under one program and provide the best allotment of resources between those projects, this standard is an invaluable tool for program and project managers alike.

The Standard for Program Management is organized as follows:

Chapter 1—Introduction: Provides guidelines for managing programs within an organization. It defines program management and related concepts, describes the program management life cycle and outlines related processes.

Chapter 2—Program Life Cycle and Organization: Describes some of the key life cycle considerations in the program management context.

Chapter 3—Program Management Processes: Identifies those Program Management Processes that have been recognized as generally accepted practices for most project portfolios most of the time.

Appendices A–H—Provides background information on the PMI Standards Program and *The Standard for Program Management* project.

Glossary—Provides clarification of key terms used in developing *The Standard for Program Management*.

Index—Gives alphabetical listings and page numbers of key topics covered in *The Standard for Program Management*.

Section I

The Program Management Framework

Chapter 1

Introduction

The Standard for Program Management provides guidelines for managing programs within an organization. It defines program management and related concepts, describes the program management life cycle and outlines related processes. This standard is an expansion of information provided in *A Guide to the Project Management Body of Knowledge* (*PMBOK® Guide*). The *PMBOK® Guide* is the accepted standard describing the process of project management and *the management of individual projects throughout their life cycle*. The *PMBOK® Guide* briefly addresses the management of multiple projects and other activities beyond the scope of managing individual projects. Although the *Organizational Project Management Maturity Model* (*OPM3®*) addresses project, program, and portfolio management, during its development, PMI determined that additional standards were needed to address program and portfolio management in detail. This standard fulfills the need for a standard for program management.

This chapter defines and explains several key terms and provides an overview of the rest of the document. It includes the following major sections:

1.1 **Purpose of** *The Standard for Program Management*
1.2 **What is a Program?**
1.3 **What is Program Management?**
1.4 **The Relationship Between Program Management and Portfolio Management**
1.5 **The Relationship Between Program Management and Project Management**
1.6 **Program Management in Organizational Planning**
1.7 **Themes of Program Management**

1.1 Purpose of *The Standard for Program Management*

The primary purpose of *The Standard for Program Management* is to describe generally recognized good practices and place program management in the context of portfolio and project management. This standard provides guidance for managing multiple programs (that is multiple projects and non-project activities within a program environment). The processes documented within this standard are generally accepted as the necessary steps to successfully manage a program. In addition this standard provides a common lexicon leading to a detailed understanding of program management among the following groups to promote efficient and effective communication and coordination:

- Project managers, to understand the role of program managers and the relationship and interface between project and program managers
- Program managers, to understand their appropriate role
- Portfolio managers, to understand the role of program managers and the relationship and interface between program and portfolio managers
- Stakeholders, to understand the role of program managers and how they engage the various stakeholder groups (e.g., users, executive management, client)
- Senior managers, to understand the role of executive sponsor as part of the program board/steering committee.

1.2 What is a Program?

A program is *a group of related projects managed in a coordinated way to obtain benefits and control not available from managing them individually.* Programs may include elements of related work (e.g., ongoing operations) outside the scope of the discrete projects in a program.

Programs and projects deliver benefits to organizations by enhancing current or developing new capabilities for the organization to use. A benefit is an outcome of actions and behaviors that provides utility to stakeholders. Benefits are gained by initiating projects and programs that invest in the organization's future. Programs, like projects, are a means of achieving organizational goals and objectives, often in the context of a strategic plan.

The terms *program* and *program management* have been in widespread use for some time and have come to mean many different things. Some organizations and industries refer to ongoing or cyclical streams of operational or functional work as programs. The recognized disciplines of operational or functional management address this type of work; therefore, this form of program is out of the scope of this standard.

Alternatively, some organizations refer to large projects as programs. The management of large individual projects or a large project that is broken into more easily managed subprojects remains within the discipline of project management, and as such, is already covered in the *PMBOK® Guide*—Third Edition. If a large project is split into multiple related projects with explicit management of the benefits, then the effort becomes a program, and this *Standard for Program Management* is applicable to managing that effort.

Programs, like projects, are a means of achieving organizational goals and objectives, often in the context of a strategic plan. Although a group of projects within a program can have discrete benefits, they often also contribute to consolidated benefits as defined by the program, as depicted in Figure 1-1.

1.3 What is Program Management?

Program management is *the centralized coordinated management of a program to achieve the program's strategic benefits and objectives.* In addition, it allows for the application of several broad management themes to help ensure the successful accomplishment of the program. These themes are: benefits management, stakeholder management, and program governance.

Managing multiple projects by means of a program allows for optimized or integrated cost, schedules, or effort; integrated or dependent deliverables across the pro-

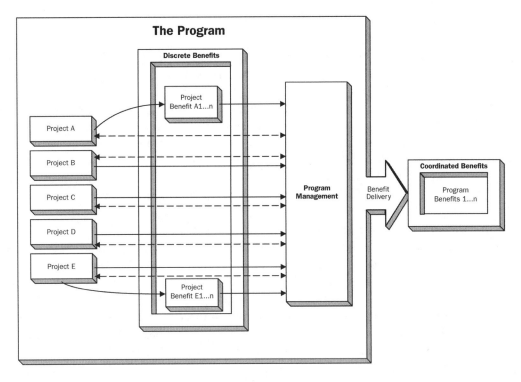

Figure 1-1. Program Benefits Management

gram, delivery of incremental benefits, and optimization of staffing in the context of the overall program's needs. Projects may be interdependent because of the collective capability that is delivered, or they may share a common attribute such as client, customer, seller, technology, or resource.

A program may link projects in various other ways, including the following:

- Interdependencies of tasks among the projects, such as meeting a new regulatory requirement for the organization or delivery of an enabling service
- Resource constraints that may affect projects within the program
- Risk mitigation activities that impact the direction or delivery of multiple projects
- Change in organizational direction that affects the work of projects and their relationships to other projects and work
- Escalation point for issues, scope changes, quality, communications management, risks, or program interfaces/dependencies.

Program management focuses on these project interdependencies and determines the optimal pacing for the program. This enables appropriate planning, scheduling, executing, monitoring, and controlling of the projects within the program. In essence, factors such as strategic benefits, coordinated planning, shared resources, interdependencies, and optimized pacing contribute to determining whether multiple projects should be managed as a program.

1.4 The Relationship Between Program Management and Portfolio Management

A portfolio is a collection of components (i.e., projects, programs, portfolios, and other work such as maintenance and ongoing operations) that are grouped together to facilitate the effective management of that work in order to meet strategic business objectives. The projects or programs of the portfolio may not necessarily be interdependent or directly related.

A portfolio always exists within an organization and it is comprised of a set of current initiatives. The initiatives may or may not be related, interdependent, or properly managed as a portfolio. The portfolio may have been created by independent efforts to authorize and launch projects without regard to strategic objectives or risks. With portfolio management, the organization is able to align the portfolio to strategic objectives, approve only components that directly support business objectives, and consider the portfolio risk as a result of the mix of components in a portfolio at any one time. Components may in fact be deferred by the organization when the risk of adding one or more of them to the current portfolio would unreasonably upset the balance and exceed the risk tolerance of the organization. As a result, the portfolio of an organization represents a snap shot of its selected components, which reflects strategic management or lack thereof and affects the strategic goals of the organization.

A portfolio is most likely one of the truest measures of an organization's intent, direction, and progress. It is where investment decisions are made, resources are allocated, and priorities are identified. If a portfolio's components are not aligned to the strategy, the organization can reasonably question why they are being undertaken.

The difference can be made clearer. Portfolio management focuses on assuring that programs and projects are viewed in priority for resource allocation (i.e., people, funding) that is consistent with and aligned to organizational strategies. Programs focus on achieving the benefits aligned with the portfolio and, subsequently, organizational objectives. Figure 1-2 depicts the sometimes complex relationship between portfolios, programs, projects, and related work.

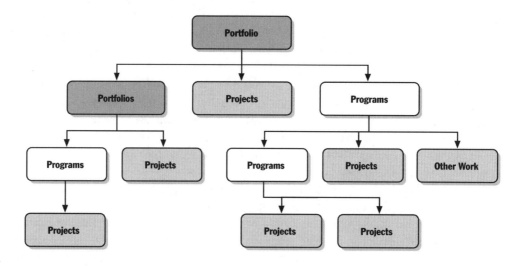

Figure 1-2. Portfolios, Programs, and Projects—High-Level View

Interactions occur between the portfolio management processes and program management processes of most Program Management Process Groups. The type of interaction and frequency will vary depending upon the needs of the Program Management Process Group.

In general, the program's Initiating and Planning Process Group will receive more inputs from the portfolio domain than will the Executing, Monitoring and Controlling, or Closing Process Groups. These inputs are often in the form of strategic goals and benefits, funding allocations, requirements, timelines, and constraints that the program team translates into the program scope, deliverables, budget, and schedule. The direction of control will be more from the portfolio domain to the program domain, whereas monitoring information will generally travel from program domain to portfolio domain. Information flowing from the program's Initiating and Planning Process Groups will typically consist of first or early views of scope development, cost estimates, and timeline estimates.

Information flowing to the portfolio domain from the program's Executing, Monitoring and Controlling, and Closing Process Groups mainly contributes to providing status information, program performance reports, budget and schedule updates, earned value cost performance reports, change requests and approved changes, and escalating issues and risks. The frequency of these interactions will be dictated by the frequency of the program's review and update cycles and the reporting requirements imposed by the portfolio management or governance team.

In summary, interactions between the program and portfolio domains fall into several categories, as follows:

- Interactions related to initiating the program
- Interactions related to providing information to the portfolio domain during the program life cycle
- Interactions related to closing the program
- Interactions related to providing changes to the program from the portfolio domain.

1.5 The Relationship Between Program Management and Project Management

During a program's life cycle, projects are initiated and the program manager oversees and provides direction and guidance to the project managers. Program managers coordinate efforts between projects but do not manage them. An essential program management responsibility is the identification, rationalization, monitoring, and control of the interdependencies between projects; dealing with the escalated issues among the projects that comprise the program; and tracking the contribution of each project and the non-project work to the consolidated program benefits.

The integrative nature of program management processes involves coordinating the processes for each of the projects or program packages. This applies through all the Process Groups of Initiating, Planning, Executing, Monitoring and Controlling, and Closing, and involves managing the processes at a level higher than those pertaining to a project. An example of this type of integration is the management of issues and risks needing resolution at the program level, because they cannot be addressed at the individual project level.

Furthermore, processes between the program and project domains can be iterative. Planning effectively for a program first requires a top-down and then a bottom-up approach. This not only helps in obtaining relevant information at appropriate levels, but helps obtain and validate buy-in from the stakeholders of a program. This type of interaction of program-level processes with project-level processes can be found during all stages of the program life cycle. An example of such an interaction can be found during schedule development, where a detailed review of the overall schedule at the project level is needed to validate information at the program level.

Similar to the interactions between the portfolio and program domains, the interactions between program and project domains tend to be cyclical. Information flows from the program to the projects in the early phases (initiating and planning) and then flows from the projects to the program in the later phases of executing, controlling and closing. The cycle is driven by the domain that is responsible for the given interaction. Table 1-1 summarizes some of the differences between portfolios, programs, and projects.

PROJECT	PROGRAMS	PORTFOLIOS
Projects have a narrow scope with specific deliverables.	Programs have a wide scope that may have to change to meet the benefit expectations of the organization.	Portfolios have a business scope that changes with the strategic goals of the organization.
The project manager tries to keep change to a minimum.	Program managers have to expect change and even embrace it.	Portfolio managers continually monitor changes in the broad environment.
Success is measured by budget, on time, and products delivered to specification.	Success is measured in terms of Return On Investment (ROI), new capabilities, and benefit delivery.	Success is measured in terms of aggregate performance of portfolio components.
Leadership style focuses on task delivery and directive in order to meet the success criteria.	Leadership style focuses on managing relationships, and conflict resolution. Program manager's need to facilitate and manage the political aspects of the stakeholder management.	Leadership style focuses on adding value to portfolio decision-making.
Project managers manage technicians, specialists, etc.	Program managers manage project managers.	Portfolio managers may manage or coordinate portfolio management staff.
Project managers are team players who motivate using their knowledge and skills.	Program managers are leaders providing vision and leadership.	Portfolio managers are leaders providing insight and synthesis.
Project managers conduct detailed planning to manage the delivery of products of the project.	Program managers create high-level plans providing guidance to projects where detailed plans are created.	Portfolio managers create and maintain necessary process and communication relative to the aggregate portfolio.
Project managers monitor and controls tasks and the work of producing the projects products.	Program managers monitor projects and ongoing work through governance structures.	Portfolio managers monitor aggregate performance and value indicators.

Table 1-1. Comparative Overview of Project, Program, and Portfolio Management

1.6 Program Management in Organizational Planning

The primary context for program management within an organization is the planning and execution of organizational plans. Programs can be thought of as the highest level at which work is directed across multiple lines of business, although programs can also support narrow single lines of business or functional areas of an organization. How much success an organization will have with program management is determined by the maturity of its policies, controls, and governance that define, communicate, and align the organization's goals.

During their life cycle, projects produce deliverables, whereas programs deliver benefits and capabilities that the organization can utilize to sustain, enhance, and deliver organizational goals.

Figure 1-3 illustrates the relationship between business initiatives in the strategic cycle and portfolios, programs and projects.

The stylized program life cycle in Figure 1-4 illustrates the nonsequential nature of program management with the mobilization of components to deliver a stream of deliverables that facilitate new operations and benefits during the program's life cycle.

Organizations address the need for change by creating strategic business initiatives to modify the organization or its products. Organizations use portfolios, programs, and projects to deliver these initiatives.

The organization must ensure that these portfolios, programs, and projects are:

- Aligned with organizational objectives or goals
- Comprised of the best mix of project investments
- Comprised of the best use of resources.

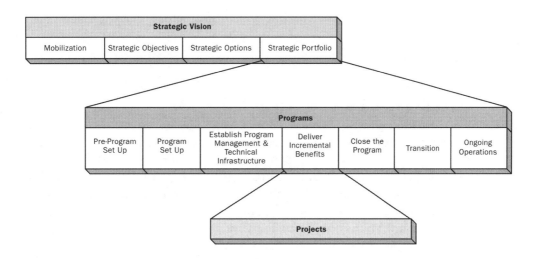

Figure 1-3. Relationships Among Portfolios, Programs, and Projects

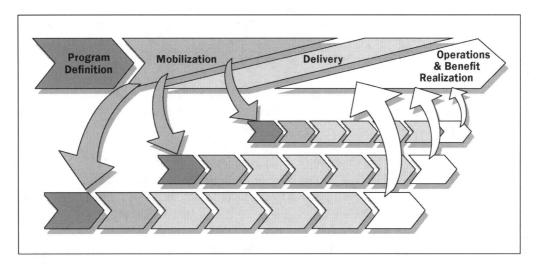

Figure 1-4. A Representative Program Life Cycle

Some organizations may not use the portfolio as a top-level structure and the program may be the entity at the top of the hierarchy of projects (see Figure 1-2).

1.7 Themes of Program Management

Organizations initiate programs to deliver benefits and accomplish agreed-upon outcomes that often affect the entire organization. The organization of the program takes this into account and balances stakeholder expectations, requirements, resources, and timing conflicts across competing projects. Throughout its life cycle, an effective program encompasses many areas, however there are three broad management themes that are key to the success of a program:

- Benefits management
- Program stakeholder management
- Program governance.

These themes run like common threads throughout the program management life cycle. The processes described in Chapter 2 on Program Life Cycle and Chapter 3 on Program Management Processes illustrate how these themes are present at all stages.

1.7.1 Benefits Management

The first theme, benefits management as applied to programs, is the definition and formalization of the expected benefits a program is intended to deliver. This includes both tangible and intangible benefits and the planning, modeling, and tracking of intermediate and final results throughout the program life cycle. Individual projects deliver results that contribute to or enable the other projects in the program to proceed, as well as contributing to the delivery of the overall program's expected benefits. Within organizations that have implemented portfolio management, the expected benefits will normally be formalized at the portfolio level before being delegated to the program for realization.

Benefits Management:
- Assesses the value and organizational impact of the program
- Identifies the interdependencies of benefits being delivered among various projects within the program
- Ensures that targeted benefits are specific, measurable, actual, realistic, and time-based
- Analyzes the potential impact of planned program changes on benefits outcome
- Assigns responsibilities and accountability for the actual benefits required from the program.

Benefits can be tangible or intangible. Tangible benefits are quantifiable and may relate to financial objectives. Intangible benefits (e.g., improved employee morale or customer satisfaction) are less easily quantified, however, most intangible benefits ultimately contribute to a tangible benefit (e.g., increased participation in an event or increased revenue results).

Benefits management begins in the early phases of a program's life cycle. The benefits realization plan, drafted early and maintained throughout all phases of a program, includes:
- Definition of each benefit and how it is to be realized
- Mapping of benefits to program outcomes
- Metrics and procedures to measure benefits
- Roles and responsibilities for benefit management
- Communications plan for benefits management
- Transition of the program into ongoing operations and benefit sustainment.

Benefits management ensures that the organization will realize and sustain the benefits from its investment in the program, even following the conclusion of the program life cycle. The program manager must see that the program transition activities provide for continued management of program benefits within the framework of ongoing operations.

The strategic planning and portfolio management processes, which identify and evaluate benefits for the organization as a whole, provide the program with a definition of the expected outcomes and resulting benefits. Figure 1-5 depicts an example of a benefits management approach that spans the program life cycle and beyond into transfer and sustainment of the benefits.

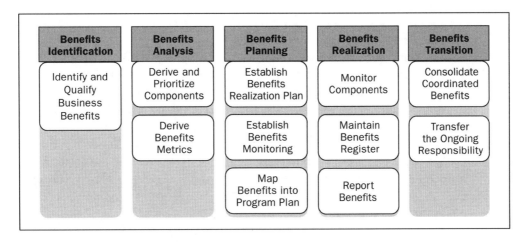

Figure 1-5. Illustrative Benefits Management Approach

1.7.2 Program Stakeholder Management

The second theme defines program stakeholders as individuals and organizations whose interests may be affected by the program outcomes, either positively or negatively. These stakeholders play a critical role in the success of any project or program. Stakeholders of a program can be internal or external to the organization. Within an organization, internal stakeholders cover all levels of the organization's hierarchy. Many stakeholders provide valuable input. Stakeholders also have the ability to influence programs—they can either help or hinder depending on the benefits or threats they see. The program manager must understand the position stakeholders may take, the way they may exert their influence, and their source of power. Where negative influence is possible, the program manager needs to ensure that the stakeholders see the benefits; something akin to marketing is often needed.

Key program stakeholders include:

- **Program Director.** The individual with executive ownership of the program or programs.
- **Program Manager.** The individual responsible for managing the program.
- **Project Managers.** The individuals responsible for managing the individual projects within the program.
- **Program Sponsor.** The individual or group who champions the program initiative, and is responsible for providing project resources and often ultimately for delivering the benefits.
- **Customer.** The individual or organization that will use the new capabilities/results of the program and derive the anticipated benefits.
- **Performing Organization.** The group that is performing the work of the program through projects.
- **Program Team Members.** The individuals performing program activities.
- **Project Team Members.** The individuals performing constituent project activities.
- **Program Management Office (PMO).** The organization responsible for defining and managing the program-related governance processes, procedures, and templates, etc.
- **Program Office.** The organization that provides support of individual program management teams or program managers by handling administrative functions centrally.
- **Program Governance Board.** The group responsible for ensuring that program goals are achieved and providing support for addressing program risks and issues.

Additional stakeholders may exist within the organization or external to it. Some examples of external stakeholders include:
- Suppliers affected by changing policies and procedures
- Governmental regulatory agencies imposing new policies
- Competitors and potential customers with an interest in the program
- Groups representing consumer, environmental, or other interests.

Stakeholders may also include individuals and groups who are not directly affected by the results of the program but maintain an interest in the initiative. Groups or individuals who are competing for limited resources or pursuing goals which conflict with those of the program should also be considered as stakeholders, since they can affect the program results.

Program stakeholder management identifies how the program will affect stakeholders (e.g., the organization's culture, current major issues, resistance or barriers to change, etc.) and then develops a communication strategy to engage the affected stakeholders, manage their expectations, and improve their acceptance of the objectives of the program.

Program stakeholder management extends beyond project stakeholder management to consider additional levels of stakeholders resulting from broader interdependencies among projects. A stakeholder management plan, combined with the communication plan, should deliver accurate, consistent, and timely information that reaches all relevant stakeholders as part of the communication process to facilitate a clear understanding of the issues. Communication planning and execution should focus on the proactive and targeted development and delivery of key messages, and engagement of key stakeholders at the right time and in the right manner.

Stakeholder management is also an important factor in implementing successful organizational change. In this context, program plans should clearly show an understanding of and integration with generally accepted methods of organizational change management. This includes identifying the key individuals who have an interest in or will be affected by the changes and ensuring they are aware of, supportive of, and part of the change process. To facilitate the change process, the program manager must communicate to stakeholders a clear vision of the need for change, as well as the initiative's specific objectives and the resources required. The program manager must also set clear goals, assess readiness, plan for the change, provide resources/support, monitor the change, obtain and evaluate feedback from those affected by the change, and address issues with people who are not fully embracing the change.

1.7.3 Program Governance

The third theme, program governance, is the process of developing, communicating, implementing, monitoring, and assuring the policies, procedures, organizational structures, and practices associated with a given program. The result is a framework for efficient and effective decision-making and delivery management focused on achieving program goals in a consistent manner, addressing appropriate risks and stakeholder requirements.

The organization's management team will want to ensure that program governance fits within the wider governance of the organization (e.g., corporate governance). As depicted in Figure 1-6, governance includes constraints and guidance offered by strategic management, related practices such as portfolio and project management, and the processes and structures that drive, monitor, and constrain the operations of the organization. A program board is a formal way to capture this executive need and forms a community or forum where the issues of the program can be managed. Although not all organizations can formalize such a structure, the practices as laid out below are common in response to the needs of program management. The program board is the group responsible for the governance of their specific program, and should be aware of any cross-program governance directives. The program board exists throughout the life of the program. The program board is sometimes referred to as the governance board or steering committee.

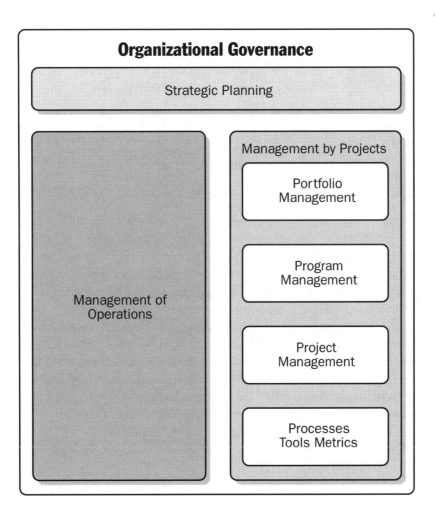

Figure 1-6. Governance Context

Program governance is concerned with controlling the organization's investment as well as monitoring the delivery of benefits as the program progresses. This control is achieved by monitoring progress reports and reviews on a routine basis and specifically at each phase in the program's life cycle. These reviews are an opportunity for senior management or their representatives to assess the performance of the program before allowing the program to move to the next phase or before the initiation of another project within the program. These reviews are discussed in Chapter 2, Section 2.2.3 (Program Governance Through Phase-Gate Reviews). Figure 1-7 displays the organizational view of a possible governance structure.

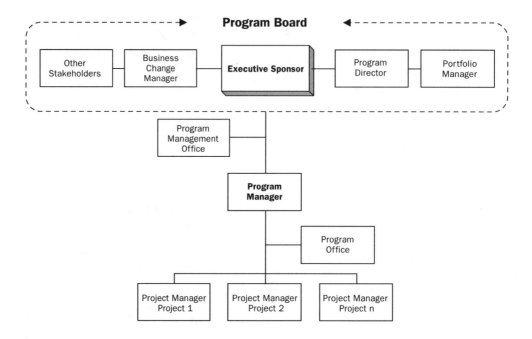

Figure 1-7. Program Governance Structure

The program board, representing the interests of the organization, provides the overarching governance and quality assurance of the program. The composition of the program board is typically a cross-functional group of senior stakeholders responsible for providing guidance and decisions regarding program direction and changes affecting the program outcomes.

Specific functions of the board include, but are not limited to, the following:
- Initiation of the program
- Approval of program plans and authorizing deviations from the plans
- Review of the program's progress, benefits delivery, and costs
- Guidance on issues that the program manager has been unable to resolve
- Assurance that resources are available for the program
- Collection of input for strategic progress reporting
- Establishment of frameworks and limits for making decisions about investments in the program
- Compliance with corporate and legal policies, procedures, standards, and requirements.

The program board is not usually a consensus committee; the executive sponsor is the key decision maker taking advice and commitments from others within the board and program management team. Each member of the board represents key internal stakeholders and may potentially include those external to the organization impacted by the program's outcomes.

The program board members do not work full time on the program; therefore, they place great reliance on the program management team.

The organization may choose to set up a program management office (PMO) with the responsibility of defining and managing the specific program-related governance processes, procedures, and templates etc., with which all programs must comply.

Organizations may then choose to have the program management office provide support to all programs. Typically, the role of the program management office is to support individual program management teams or program managers by handling administrative functions centrally.

Figure 1-8 illustrates the hierarchy of governance and the deliverables that the roles are expected to generate for the organization.

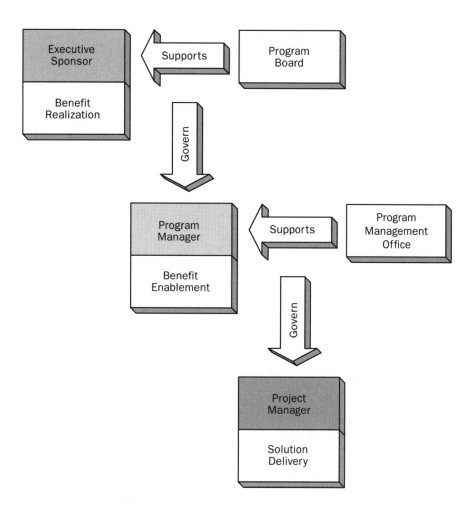

Figure 1-8. Governance Framework

CHAPTER 2

Program Life Cycle and Organization

As defined in Chapter 1, programs and program management exist within a strategic context and operate as strategy implementation vehicles. The program manager must understand this wider context to be able to adapt the life cycle model and program benefits to satisfy the corresponding requirements assigned to the program.

This chapter describes some of the key life cycle considerations in the program management context. The topics include:

2.1 Program Life Cycle
2.2 Program Themes Across the Program Life Cycle
2.3 Program Management Life Cycle Phases

2.1 Program Life Cycle

Organizations and their project managers recognize that current best practice in project control involves breaking the project into discrete stages or phases. The management of programs has the same requirement. To ensure effective program control, the program moves through discrete, though often overlapping phases. These phases facilitate program governance, enhanced control, and coordination of program and project resources and overall risk management.

Program life cycles serve to manage outcomes and benefits, as contrasted with project life cycles, which serve to produce deliverables. Project products deliver capabilities to the organization, while the program manages and accrues the corresponding benefits during the Delivering the Incremental Benefits phase as shown in Figure 2-1 and explained in detail in Section 2.3.4. It should be noted that this is the phase in which the main effort and time of the program are expended as the benefits are progressively delivered. As such, it is of an iterative nature with internal links to project and program governances. To ensure that the program delivers and tracks the expected benefits, there is usually senior management oversight of a program by means of phase-gate reviews as shown in Figure 2-2, in order to comply with program governance as described in Section 1.7.3 in the previous chapter. In the context of a program,

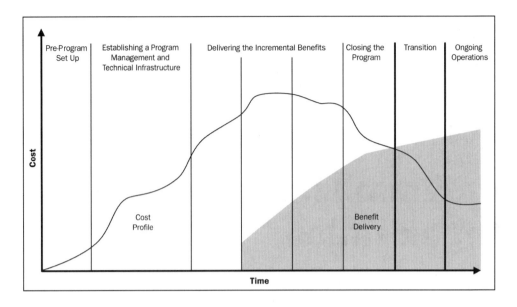

Figure 2-1. Typical Cost and Benefit Profiles Across the Generic Program Life Cycle

some projects may produce benefits that can be realized immediately whereas other projects may deliver capabilities that must be integrated with the capabilities delivered by other projects before the associated benefits can be realized.

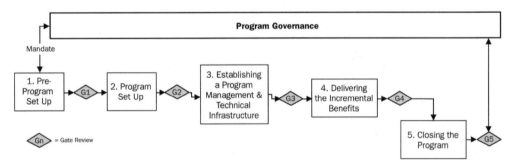

Figure 2-2. A Representative Program Life Cycle

The type of program being managed may influence a program's life cycle; however, the major life cycle phases and their deliverables will remain similar. An example of this is pharmaceutical or medical device manufacturers who have to conduct extensive clinical trials (projects) during and after a product has been developed. The regulators for these industries also review the organization's use of risk management to assess potential flaws in their products. Each of these steps will normally be run as one or more projects, or, if required, as a program.

The key distinctions between program and project life cycles are:

- Programs often have an extended life cycle as some projects transition to operations while other projects are only just being initiated.
- Projects generate discrete deliverables at the completion of their life cycle, and the resulting benefits subsequently flow into the program.
- The capabilities delivered by several of the program's projects may need to be integrated in order to provide some or all of the program's benefits.

The *PMBOK® Guide*—Third Edition addresses the use of a project life cycle to assist in the control and management of the project deliverables. Within a program there are several projects, each following its own project life cycle. In fact, each project could use a different life cycle model, depending on the type of project. In such cases, the program manager may define a project life cycle model to create a common language among stakeholders and facilitate reporting and monitoring the status of all projects within the program.

An example of this could be:

Hardware System Project	Information System Project	Standard Project Life Cycle
• Requirements Survey	• Inception	• Initial Investigation
• Capacity Planning	• Elaboration	• Detailed Design
• Construct & Test	• Construction & Testing	• Construct & Test
• Occupation & Trial	• Transition	• Trial
• Switch Over	• Deployment	• Release

Table 2-1. Example of a Project Life Cycle Model

2.2 Program Themes Across the Program Life Cycle

As introduced in Chapter 1, three themes permeate all activities of a program: benefits management, stakeholder management, and program governance. These themes evolve over time and require a program manager's focus throughout each phase of the program's life cycle.

2.2.1 Benefits Management and the Program Life Cycle

The program life cycle is designed not only to comply with the needs of corporate governance, but also to ensure that the expected benefits are realized in a predictable and coordinated manner. Benefits management requires the establishment of processes and measures for tracking and assessing benefits throughout the program life cycle. In fact, the management of program benefits has a life cycle of its own, which runs parallel to that of the program. Benefits management evolves as the program evolves through its phases. This relationship between program life cycle and the benefits management life cycle is illustrated in Figure 2-3.

To be successful, benefits management must begin when the program is initiated, in the Pre-Program Set Up and Program Set Up life cycle phases. There should be clear definition and agreement among stakeholders on the factors contributing to benefits, as well as a supporting structure and processes to help plan, manage, measure, track, and realize the benefits. The benefits expected from each project should be defined in the project business case before the project is initiated, together with the benefit tracking and assessment processes.

The Program Management and Technical Infrastructure phases should be established in such a way as to be capable of recording, tracking, and evaluating benefits in accordance with the benefits definition and assessment processes defined in the preceding phase.

During program end-of-phase reviews and at the Closing Program phase, benefits management includes reporting planned versus actual benefits at the current point

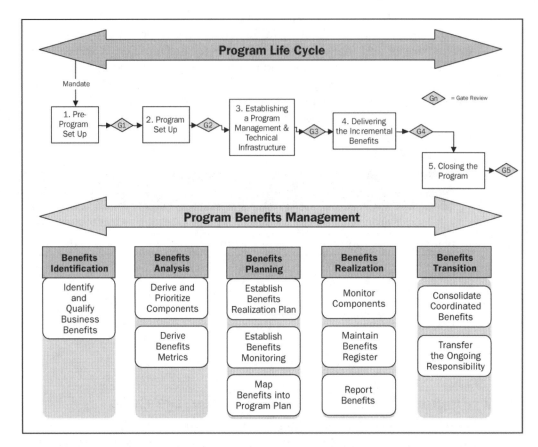

Figure 2-3. Program Life Cycle and Benefits Management

in time as well as the forecast for their ongoing value, reasons for any deviations, and recommendations on how gaps can be bridged.

2.2.2 Stakeholder Management

As described in Chapter 1 (Section 1.7.2), program stakeholder management must carefully consider the interests and concerns of the often extensive stakeholder list in order to ensure program success. Program stakeholder management is a required function that starts with the identification and analysis of all stakeholders and spans all the life cycle phases of a program.

Each stakeholder can play a significant role in the success of any program. For this reason, the program management team must identify stakeholders early in the program life cycle, and then actively manage stakeholder expectations throughout all of the life cycle phases to ensure their continued support of the program.

In many instances, a change to the program environment can add or remove stakeholders; the program manager must manage the stakeholder list throughout the lifetime of the program and take appropriate actions to handle expected or actual changes.

2.2.3 Program Governance Through Phase-Gate Reviews

Program governance, as explained in Section 1.7.3 of Chapter 1, focuses on the oversight of programs by a steering committee or governance board. The use of additional tools, such as pre-defined milestones or phase-gate reviews, can complement the governance structure. The use in this way of a formal program methodology constitutes a generally accepted practice for applying governance through a program.

The phase-gate reviews are generally focused on strategic alignment, investment appraisal, monitoring and control of opportunities and threats, benefit assessment, and the monitoring of the program outcomes. In cases where the program was initiated as part of a portfolio, these reviews will be carried out within the context of the corresponding portfolio.

The phase-gate reviews, shown in Figure 2-2, are a recommended approach to aiding program control and program management, as well as facilitating program governance. Phase-gate reviews are carried out at key decision points in the program life cycle. The purpose of phase-gate reviews is to provide an objective check against the exit criteria of a completed phase to determine readiness to proceed to the next phase in the program life cycle. Phase-gate reviews also provide an opportunity to assess the program with respect to a number of strategic and quality-related criteria including:

- Program and its constituent projects are still aligned with the organization's strategy
- Expected benefits are in line with the original business plan
- Level of risk remains acceptable to the organization
- Identified generally accepted good practices are being followed.

Phase-gate reviews are often based upon the core investment decisions within the life cycle. The focus of each phase-gate review is specific to the phase just completed by the program. Each phase-gate review functions as a "go" or "no-go" decision point on the program as a whole. In the case of phase-gate G5, shown throughout the graphics here, it is a convention to indicate confirmation of program closure.

Phase-gate reviews do not substitute for periodic program performance reviews that assess performance against expected outcomes and against the need to realize and sustain program benefits into the long term.

2.3 Program Management Life Cycle Phases

This section defines the phases of the generic life cycle introduced in Figure 2-2. These phases will apply to most programs most of the time. Between the phases are predefined milestones or phase-gate reviews, as introduced in the previous section. The gate numbers shown correspond to the five previously mentioned gates.

2.3.1 Program Governance Across the Life Cycle

While it is not, strictly speaking, a phase in the program management life cycle, this process spans all of the program life cycle phases. Program governance—using the governance mechanisms identified in Sections 1.7.3 on Program Governance and 2.2.3 on Governance through phase-gate review—monitors the progress of the program and the delivery of the coordinated benefits from its component projects.

Program governance provides an appropriate organizational structure and the policies and procedures to support program delivery through formal program reviews facilitated by the regular and phase-gate-based oversight of deliverables, performance, risks, and issues by the program board.

Program governance is fulfilled through the following roles:

- **Executive Sponsor.** Responsible for creating an environment that will ensure program success
- **Program Director.** Possesses executive ownership of the program policies

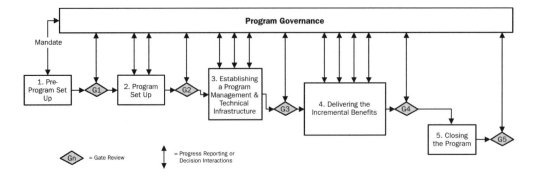

Figure 2-4. Program Governance

- **Program Board or Steering Committee.** Empowered to make decisions regarding program scope, budget, and schedules and to resolve escalated issues and risks
- **Program Manager.** Supported by any associated program office and responsible for conducting appropriate program management activities, as outlined in Chapter 3
- **Project Managers.** Responsible for providing accurate and timely status reports and for reporting and escalating risks and issues as they are identified.

Program governance activities are conducted through all phases of the program life cycle and require organizations to establish and enforce policies that address the following:
- Common procedures for all projects within the program
- Appropriate controls to ensure consistent application of procedures
- Approach for developing and documenting program assumptions and decisions
- Approach for managing program change
- Quantifiable measures for evaluating the success of individual projects and the program
- Common practices for capturing risks, issues, benefit measurements, and lessons learned.

These policies are most often created by the program office with input from the steering committee and project teams. The policies provide a framework for all program activities.

Phase-gate reviews provide an opportunity for senior management to ensure the initiative remains viable and continues to support the organization's strategy. These reviews can also provide an opportunity for senior management to review critical program risks and issues. At each phase-gate review, the program may be approved to go forward to the next phase or may be cancelled. Additional review gates can be defined during the longest phase of the program, the delivering the incremental benefits phase, to monitor the progress of the constituent projects.

2.3.2 Phase One: Pre-Program Set Up

The primary objective of the Pre-Program Set Up phase is to establish a firm foundation of support and approval for the program.

In program and project management life cycles, there is a business-based selection process that determines whether an organization will approve a program/project. A strategic decision-making body in the form of a program board, portfolio management group or executive sponsor of the program (usually a senior executive or portfolio manager) initiates the program with a mandate or program brief detailing the strategic objectives and benefits that the program is expected to deliver. This selection process may range from a very informal one to a more formal, standardized approach. As shown in *OPM3®*, the more mature an organization is in terms of program management, the more likely it is to have a formalized selection process.

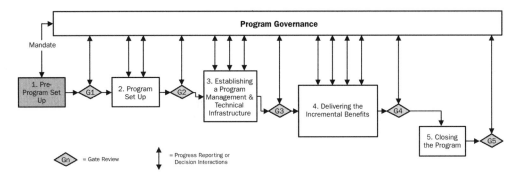

Figure 2-5. Pre-Program Set Up

The pre-program set up phase focuses on the preparation and navigation through the selection process and typically consists of several activities:
- Understanding the strategic value of the proposed business change
- Identifying the key decision makers/stakeholders in the program selection process and their expectations and interests
- Defining the program objectives and their alignment with the organization's strategic objectives
- Developing a high-level business case demonstrating an understanding of the needs, feasibility and justification of the program
- Securing approval for the program charter by getting signatures of the key stakeholders
- Appointing the program manager by the program board
- Developing a plan to initiate the program.

Program management provides a focused effort to achieve the strategic objectives of the organization. Programs are more strategic in nature than projects. As a result, in the Pre-Program Set Up phase, there is a significant need to show how the program would map to and deliver the strategic objectives through alignment of its constituent projects. Programs are generally undertaken by organizations as a catalyst for some level of change. In this case, program plans should clearly show an understanding of and integration with generally accepted methods of organizational change management.

During this phase, the program manager or executive sponsor also needs to consider and answer the question of why the expected business benefits would be best realized through a program rather than a project. There should be a clear indication of the *type* of program being recommended and the criteria used to arrive at the recommendation. The rationale used could include considerations as:
- Shared resources across projects
- Program duration
- Participation across corporate entities
- Dependencies on deliverables between projects to create a set of benefits.
  The stakeholders at this stage are:

- Those who are in a position to influence the selection of the program for approval or
- Those who are in a position to influence the success of the program if it is selected (i.e., those impacted by the results of the program).

The information required, and the orientation of the selection committee, may be significantly different from those of the stakeholders who will eventually benefit from the program. This fact may have an impact on the analysis and documentation required at this phase.

Once the strategic area to be addressed is clearly understood, and the stakeholders with whom communication must be established are identified, then a high-level approach or plan needs to be developed. This plan must show that the program manager clearly understands the stimuli that triggered the program, the program objectives, and how the objectives align to the organization. The high-level plan should include a clear statement of the following program components:

- **Mission**—why the program is important and what it needs to achieve
- **Vision**—what the end state will look like, how it will benefit the organization
- **Values**—how the program will evaluate necessary tradeoffs and balance the decisions to be made.

The selection criteria and materials to be provided may range from vague and informal to very detailed, specific, and formal. Typically, the following factors are considered in selecting and approving programs:

- Total available resources (i.e., funding, equipment or people)
- Preliminary budget estimates required for this program
- Benefits analysis, which identifies and plans for their realization
- Strategic fit within the organization's long-term goals
- Risks inherent in this program.
  The results from this stage of the life cycle are:
- Approval from a governing board to proceed to the next phase
- Program charter that documents the vision, key objectives, expected benefits, constraints of the program, and any assumptions to be used for planning (key input)
- Assigned program manager
- Identification and commitment of key resources needed for planning
- A plan for the program set up phase.

2.3.3 Phase Two: Program Set Up

At this stage, the program has passed the first phase-gate review (G1) and has received "approval in principle" from a selection committee to proceed to program set up. A program manager has been identified and the key input into this phase—a charter defining high-level scope, objectives, visions, and constraints—has been generated.

The purpose of the Program Set Up phase is to continue to develop the foundation for the program by now building a detailed "roadmap" that provides direction on how the program will be managed and defines its key deliverables.

The desired outcome of this phase is approval authorizing execution of the program management plan. To achieve that outcome, the detailed program management plan contains answers to the following questions:

- What are the deliverables and when will they be ready?
- How much will it cost?
- What are the risks and issues?
- What dependencies, assumptions, and constraints are included?
- How will the program be managed/executed?

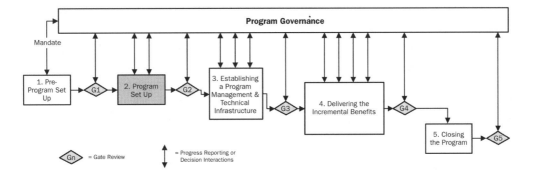

Figure 2-6. Program Set Up

If the program's components have not already been defined, this phase will determine the components that need to be included with the program, as well as any feasibility studies that may need to be conducted to address program issues. Activities in this second phase could include:

- Aligning the mission, vision, and values for the program with the organization's objectives
- Developing an initial detailed cost and schedule plan for setting up the program and outline plans for the remainder of the program
- Conducting feasibility studies, where applicable, to assess the proposed program for technical and economic feasibility, as well as ethical feasibility or acceptability
- Establishing rules for make/buy decisions as well as those for selecting subcontractors to support the program
- Developing a program architecture that maps out how the projects within the program will deliver the capabilities that result in the required benefits
- Developing a business case for each project in the program which addresses the technical, investment and regulatory/legislative factors which may pertain to each project
- Communicating with stakeholders and getting support.

Key results from this stage of the life cycle revolve around the program-level Planning Processes and include:

- Scope definition and planning
- Activity definition and sequencing
- Duration estimates
- Schedule
- Procurement of external resources
- Internal/external resources/staffing allocation
- Cost estimates/budgeting
- Risk management consolidation
- Constituent component identification and definition
- Approval of the program management plan, based upon the individual business cases and supporting feasibility studies
- Identification of preliminary program team.

2.3.4 Phase Three: Establish Program Management and Technical Infrastructure

The purpose of this phase is to establish an infrastructure that will support the program and its constituent projects as they deliver the expected benefits for the program.

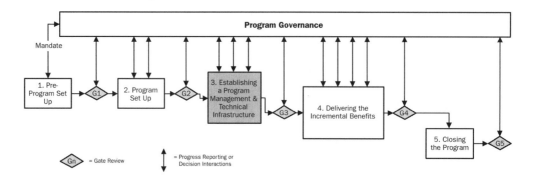

Figure 2-7. Establish the Program Infrastructure

Once the program has passed the second phase-gate review (G2), the program manager has a mandate to execute the program as defined by its roadmap, subject to organizational boundaries beyond which the program manager would need to reaffirm/ realign the program. In this phase, the program manager and the program team need to establish the structure in which work will occur along with the technical infrastructure to facilitate that work. More so than projects, programs usually have a supporting infrastructure in place, including the following:
- Program-specific governance areas such as processes and procedures
- Program-specific tools such as Enterprise Resource Planning (ERP), program tracking tools, time/expense reporting, software development tools, benefit measurement, monitoring and tracking, etc.
- Program facilities.

The program requires an organization to support the controlling and monitoring of the program and its projects and to make decisions for the program. The program organizational structure typically consists of:
- **Program Board.** Representing the interests of the organization, possibly supported by a Program Management Office that is responsible for managing cross-program governance.
- **Program Manager.** Representing the program team, including the corresponding project managers, possibly supported by a Program Office to assist the program manager in cross-project governance.
  The key roles within this structure are:
- **Executive Sponsor.** Has primary responsibility to the business for delivery of benefits and who sits with the program board to make business decisions about the program.
- **Program Director.** Has executive ownership of the program. The program director and executive sponsor could be the same person.
- **Program Manager.** Responsible for managing and representing the program.
- **Program Team.** Responsible to develop program-level benefits.
- **Program Office.** Supports the program manager and program team.

The program structure and the relationships within the structure are defined in the program framework and customized in the program charter and plan. The key results from this phase include:
- Program team staffing
- Program office to support the program
- Program governance mechanism with approval and reporting procedures
- Program control framework for monitoring and controlling both the projects and the measurement of benefits within the program
- Facilities and other required infrastructure to support the program
- IT systems and communication technologies with the necessary support arrangements to sustain the program throughout its life cycle.

2.3.5 Phase Four: Deliver the Benefits

The purpose of this phase is to initiate the component projects of the program and coordinate the deliverables to create the incremental benefits.

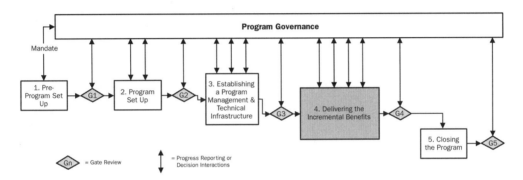

Figure 2-8. Deliver the Benefits

At this point in the program's life cycle, the program has passed another phase-gate review (G3) and the core work of the program—through its components—begins. This phase is therefore iterative and can be of unlimited duration, since the activities described below are repeated as often as required and the benefits are achieved in a cumulative manner. The phase ends only when the planned benefits of the program have been achieved or a decision is made to terminate the program for any other reason.

The program management team is responsible for managing this group of related projects in a consistent and coordinated way in order to achieve incremental benefits that could not be obtained by managing the projects as stand-alone efforts. The following activities are performed during this phase:
- Establishing a project governance structure to monitor and control the projects
- Initiating projects in order to meet program objectives
- Managing the transition from the "as-is" state to the "to-be" or target state
- Ensuring project managers adhere to established project management methodologies
- Ensuring project deliverables meet their business/technical requirements
- Analyzing progress to plan
- Identifying environmental changes which may impact the program management plan or anticipated benefits
- Ensuring that common activities and dependencies between projects or other programs in the portfolio are coordinated
- Identifying risks and ensuring appropriate mitigation actions have been taken

- Identifying issues and ensuring corrective actions are taken
- Coordinating the efficient use of resources across the program and project activities
- Reviewing change requests and authorizing additional work as appropriate
- Setting thresholds for corrective action when realized benefits are not delivered per expectations
- Communicating with stakeholders and the program governance board.

The program manager or, for larger programs, the program management office reviews the efforts by the constituent project teams. It will be up to the program manager/PMO to determine the key intersections and critical interfaces of the project and the program.

2.3.6 Phase Five: Close the Program
The purpose of this phase is to execute a controlled closedown of the program.

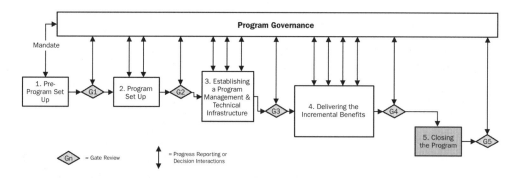

Figure 2-9. Close the Program

The last phase of a program begins after a phase-gate review (G4). All program work is completed and benefits are accruing. The activities in this phase lead to the shut down of the program organization and infrastructure as well as the transition of artifacts, benefits monitoring, and on-going operations to other groups.

There are key activities that must be executed when a program arrives at the end of its life cycle to ensure that the closure is smooth and safe.
- Review status of benefits with the stakeholders and program sponsor.
- Disband the program organization.
- Disband the program team; ensure arrangements are in place for appropriate re-deployment of all human resources.
- Dismantle the infrastructure; ensure arrangements are in place for appropriate redeployment of all physical resources (e.g., facilities, equipment, etc.).
- Provide customer support assuring that guidance and maintenance will be provided in the case that an issue arises or a defect is detected after the release; this assurance is generally defined by contract.
- Document lessons learned in the organizational database so they can be referenced in the future by similar programs. Lessons learned are generally expressed as weaknesses or areas to improve and as strengths and best practices of the performing organization to be utilized in the future.
- Provide feedback and recommendations on changes identified during the program's life but beyond the scope of the program that may benefit the organization to pursue.
- Store and index all program-related documents to facilitate reuse in the future.
- Manage any required transition to operations.

Section II

The Standard for Program Management

Chapter 3   Program Management Processes

Chapter 3

Program Management Processes

Program management is the centralized coordinated management of a program to achieve the program's strategic objectives and benefits. Good program management requires visionary, entrepreneurial, and motivational zeal, combined with sound management processes.

The process definitions and terminology at the program level are very similar to the processes at the project level. However, program management processes address issues at a higher level and involve less detailed project-level analysis. The program level is configured to resolve issues between projects and to enable a synergistic approach, so as to deliver program benefits. Like project management processes, program management processes require coordination with other functional groups in the organization as well as stakeholder management in general—but in a broader context.

A guiding rule for applying program management processes is to ensure that the program manager effectively delegates authority, autonomy, and responsibility for day-to-day management of the projects to the designated project managers.

Program management processes are primarily integrative in that they coordinate the outputs of various projects to derive the desired program outcomes. For this reason, the program management processes can be mapped in terms of the various Knowledge Areas outlined in the *PMBOK® Guide*—Third Edition. This mapping is described in Section 3.10.

This chapter includes the following major sections:

3.1 Themes in the Program Management Life Cycle

In Chapter 1 of this standard, three major themes in program management are identified and described. In this chapter, the processes that support the themes are described.

3.1.1 Benefits Management

Benefits management is one of the three major themes in program management, since programs are created to produce benefits that would not otherwise be realized. Benefits management assesses the value and organizational impact of the program's benefits, identifies the interdependencies of benefits being delivered among various projects within the program, and assigns responsibilities and accountability for the actual realization of benefits from the program.

A benefits realization plan is a critical component of the Initiate Program Process that includes: intended interdependencies between benefits, alignment with the strategic goals of the organization, benefit delivery scheduling, metrics and measurement, responsibility for delivery of the final and intermediate benefits within the program, and benefit realization. The interdependencies, benefit delivery scheduling, and responsibility for delivery, lie within the program management domain.

Expected benefits should be defined in the business case on which the program is based. The benefits realization plan for the program is based on this information and is the main output from the Initiate Program Process. In this case, where the program is launched as a component of a portfolio, the benefits realization plan should be available from the portfolio management domain or a strategic planning function. This plan is the basis for the program management plan and helps to determine how benefits will subsequently be realized, and provides a baseline for tracking progress and reporting any variances.

3.1.2 Stakeholder Management

As stated in Chapter 1, stakeholders play a critical role in the success of the program. This role is recognized and addressed throughout the processes defined in this chapter. The program stakeholders' expectations need to be taken into account and managed in all of the Program Management Process Groups from initiation through closure. A stakeholder analysis and management plan needs to be produced as the program is being initiated.

3.1.3 Program Governance

Chapter 2 of this standard provides the life cycle focus on program governance, whereas Chapter 3 establishes the processes by which program governance is implemented. Program governance is a combination of the activities of a program board, or other entity with oversight of the program, and the program manager and program team, who accomplish program governance by means of the program management processes.

The processes of program management and their outputs and results are necessary for governance to occur, but program governance itself operates in a manner external to the program. Governance controls the program, and therefore bridges the program life cycle and the program management processes.

3.2 Program Management Process Groups

This section identifies and describes the five Program Management Process Groups. These Process Groups align to those defined in the *PMBOK® Guide*—Third Edition and are independent of application areas or industry focus.

These Process Groups are not linear and do overlap. Interaction occurs both within a Process Group and between Process Groups. It is important to note that these Process Groups do not bear any direct relationship to phases of a program life cycle. In fact, one or more processes from each Process Group will normally be executed at least once in every phase of a program life cycle. The five Program Management Process Groups are briefly discussed below:

- **Initiating Process Group.** Defines and authorizes the program or a project within the program and produces the program benefits statement and benefits realization plan for the program.
- **Planning Process Group.** Plans the best alternative courses of action to deliver the benefits and scope that the program was undertaken to address.
- **Executing Process Group.** Integrates projects, people, and other resources to carry out the plan for the program and deliver the program's benefits.
- **Monitoring and Controlling Process Group.** Requires that the program and its component projects be monitored against the benefit delivery expectations and that their progress be regularly measured, to identify variances from the program management plan. This Process Group also coordinates corrective actions to be taken, when necessary, to achieve program benefits.
- **Closing Process Group.** Formalizes acceptance of a product, service, or benefit/result; brings the program or program component (e.g., project) to an orderly end.

3.3 Common Program Management Process Components

Each of the program management processes may have components (inputs, outputs, and tools and techniques) that are unique to that process, but there are also components that are common to many processes throughout the Program Management Process Groups. Among these are inputs and outputs such as assumptions, constraints, historical information, lessons learned and supporting details, and controls such as policies, procedures, and reviews.

Instead of repeating these components in many process descriptions, they have been described and explained below in terms of how they apply to the program management process approach in general.

3.3.1 Inputs Common to Program Management Processes

There are a number of inputs that are common to most program management processes. Generally, the common inputs fall into a category that can be considered common knowledge within the organization. For example, assumptions or constraints could be inputs to almost any process. Some of the inputs common to many program management processes are presented below. In addition, others can be identified and observed while studying the program management processes.

.1 Assumptions (Input and Output)

Assumptions are factors that, for planning purposes, are considered true, real, or certain. Assumptions affect all aspects of program planning and are part of the progressive elaboration of the program. Program teams frequently identify, document and validate assumptions as part of their planning. Due to their uncertainty, assumptions generally involve a degree of risk.

.2 Constraints (Input)

Constraints are factors that limit the program team's options. They are factors external to the program that will limit the flexibility of the program manager. Constraints generally fall in the categories of time, cost, resources, or specific deliverables.

.3 Historical Information (Input)

Previous programs can be a source of lessons learned and best practices for a new program. This is particularly true for programs where a substantial amount of work is done by virtual means or when the work involves multicultural interaction. Historical information includes all artifacts, metrics, risks, and estimations from previous programs and projects that are pertinent to the current program. Historical information describing the successes, failures and lessons learned on past programs with respect to integrating multiple projects is especially important to program planning and management.

.4 Organizational Process Assets (Input)

Organizational process assets, sometimes called a Process Asset Library (PAL), are composed of a set of formal and informal program management process-related plans, policies, procedures, and guidelines that are developed, documented, and institutionalized by the organization. These assets may also include an organization's knowledge bases, such as lessons learned and historical information. Assets may exist as paper documents or in electronic form in an automated repository.

3.3.2 Outputs Common to Program Management Processes

There are also a number of outputs which are common among the processes. For example, assumptions and lessons learned could be outputs from almost any process. Some of the outputs common to many program management processes are presented below. In addition, others can be identified and observed while studying the program management processes.

.1 Lessons Learned (Output)

Lessons learned include causes of variances from the program management plan, corrective actions taken and their outcomes, risk mitigations and other information of value to management and stakeholders of future programs. Lessons learned should be identified and documented throughout the program management processes, and flow to the Close Program Process for analysis and archiving.

.2 Supporting Details (Output)

Supporting details vary by process and program size. Supporting details consist of documentation and information not included in formal program artifacts but deemed necessary to the successful management of the program.

.3 Information Requests (Output)

Requests for information on various aspects of a program are initiated continuously and frequently by the program's external and internal stakeholders and are outputs from many of its program management processes. Information requests flow to the Information Distribution Process, which creates the appropriate responses as outputs.

3.4 Initiating Process Group

Initiation of a program occurs as the result of a strategic plan, a strategic initiative to fulfill an initiative within a portfolio, or as the result of a decision to bid for a contract from an external customer. There may be a number of activities performed before the Initiate Program Process, resulting in the development of concepts (for products or services), scope frameworks, initial requirements, timelines, deliverables, and guidelines as to acceptable costs.

Program funding is required to support the program through the initiation and planning phases until cost and budget estimating is complete. Significant resources can be required for these early activities.

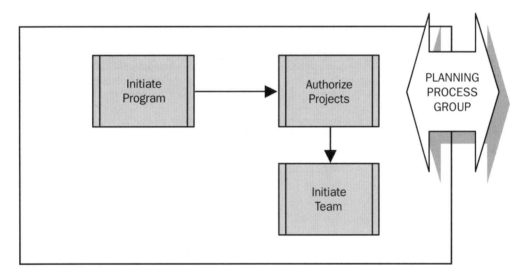

Figure 3-1. Initiating Process Group

3.4.1 Initiate Program

Often the starting point for a program is an organizational concept for a future state to fit in with a future organizational environment. Initially, this concept may be inadequately defined and the purpose of Initiate Program is to provide a process that helps define the scope and benefit expectations of the program. Initiate Program also ensures that authorization and initiation of the program are linked to the organization's ongoing work and strategic priorities.

Candidates for program status include project work as well as non-project work, such as new investments and ongoing operations. Initiating a program can entail configuring or grouping proposed projects and existing projects into a program based on specific benefit delivery or other criteria. Initiate Program also requires formal acceptance of the program scope from the stakeholders. Such acceptance acknowledges the necessity of the program as a way to achieve the desired portfolio or strategic benefits. Formal acceptance usually means each stakeholder signs off on the scope document.

Initiate Program generally calls for order-of-magnitude estimates of scope, effort, and cost. Such estimates are often called feasibility studies or concept development. A feasibility study may or may not occur before a formal initiation of a program. This will depend on the culture of the organization and the type of program under consideration. In either case, the results of the activities are used as inputs to one or more of the Initiating and Planning Processes.

The Initiate Program Process takes into account the organization's strategic plan and its business needs, as documented in a business case and investment analysis, which are developed externally to the program domain. The business case and investment analysis, then define the way in which those business needs will be achieved.

Programs are typically chartered and authorized by an organizational executive committee, steering committee, or a portfolio management body. Key outputs of this process include the program charter and preliminary scope statement. The program charter links the program to the ongoing work of the organization. The charter often contains the vision statement that defines the desired organizational end state to follow for successful completion of the program, and is used as the vehicle to authorize the program. The preliminary scope statement includes objectives and high-level deliverables of the program.

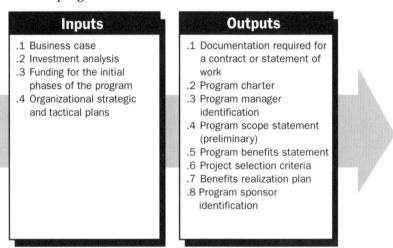

Inputs

.1 Business case
.2 Investment analysis
.3 Funding for the initial phases of the program
.4 Organizational strategic and tactical plans

Outputs

.1 Documentation required for a contract or statement of work
.2 Program charter
.3 Program manager identification
.4 Program scope statement (preliminary)
.5 Program benefits statement
.6 Project selection criteria
.7 Benefits realization plan
.8 Program sponsor identification

Table 3-1. Initiate Program: Inputs and Outputs

3.4.2 Authorize Projects

Authorize Projects is the process of performing the program management activities to initiate a component within the program. This process can occur during any program phase except closing. The timing to initiate a project is usually controlled by the program management plan. In some cases, the program team may discover the need to initiate a project that was not previously planned.

The Authorize Projects Process at the program level includes:
- Developing a business case that will secure funding for and allocating budget to the project
- Ensuring that a project manager is assigned
- Communicating project-related information to the stakeholders

- Initiating a governance structure that will monitor and track benefit delivery and progress of the project at the program level.

In some cases, the program manager will be the sponsor for the project.

Authorize Projects may trigger the redeployment of human and other resources from one project or activity to another. This is managed at the program level and may require other program process activity if the managers of the releasing project are unable or unwilling to release the resources required. Finally, all program-level documentation and records dealing with the project must be updated to reflect the new status of the projects in question.

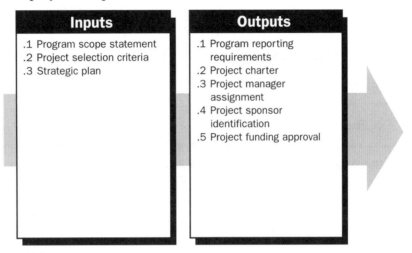

Inputs	Outputs
.1 Program scope statement .2 Project selection criteria .3 Strategic plan	.1 Program reporting requirements .2 Project charter .3 Project manager assignment .4 Project sponsor identification .5 Project funding approval

Table 3-2. Authorize Projects: Inputs and Outputs

3.4.3 Initiate Team

The Initiate Team Process gets needed human resources assigned to and working on the program. The program management team is responsible for ensuring that the human resources selected will be able to achieve the program requirements. This responsibility typically involves designating personnel from within the organization to be assigned to the program team. However, other human resources may be obtained to augment the program, through recruiting new employees, retaining consulting staff to support the program or incorporating human resources from subcontractors and teaming partners.

Initiate Team commences in conjunction with the Initiate Program Process and kick-off meeting. The objective is to formalize the appointment of the program manager by the program sponsor and to put in place the key personnel who will comprise the core program team. At this point in the program life cycle, the role of the program manager and core program team is to accomplish the tasks necessary to position the program to commence the Planning Processes. Some members of the core program team may be assigned to the program only to participate in the initiation or start-up of the program and may be replaced by permanent staff during the Resource Planning and Acquire Program Team Processes.

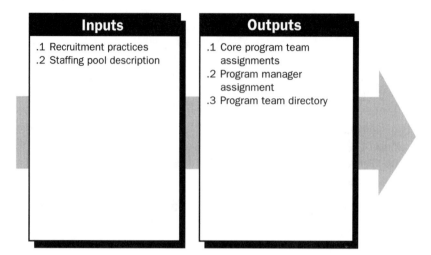

Inputs	Outputs
.1 Recruitment practices .2 Staffing pool description	.1 Core program team assignments .2 Program manager assignment .3 Program team directory

Table 3-3. Initiate Team: Inputs and Outputs

3.5 Planning Process Group

The Planning Process Group contains the processes needed to lay the groundwork for the program and position it for successful execution. These processes involve formalizing the scope of the work to be accomplished by the program and identifying the deliverables that will satisfy the program's goals and deliver its benefits.

The key program-level deliverable that is created by the Planning Processes is the program management plan, which defines the tactical means by which the program will be carried out. Included in the program management plan, either as components within the document or as subsidiary plans, are the plans that drive the basic elements of managing the program. These plans include and address:

- Organization of the program
- Program work breakdown structure (PWBS) that formalizes the program scope in terms of deliverables and the work needed to produce those deliverables/benefits via the projects
- Internal and external resources required for performing the work defined in the PWBS
- All aspects of scope, technology, risks and costs
- Program schedule that establishes the timeline for program milestones and deliverables
- Program budget that defines the monetary plan for the program in terms of outlays of funds over the program life cycle and the purposes to which those funds will be applied
- Means by which the required quality of the program deliverables will be assured
- Plans for defining metrics and systems to track benefit delivery, realization and sustainment
- Communications with stakeholders both internal and external to the program
- Approach and methodology to be followed to manage risks associated with the program
- Procurement management plan created during the first iteration of the Plan Program Purchases and Acquisitions Process, and then updated as needed while performing the Executing Processes.
- Plans for procurement of facilities, goods, services and other external resources needed to accomplish the program, and to manage contractual vehicles for procurement
- Interrelationships between projects and non-project tasks within the program, between the program and its projects or with factors external to the program.

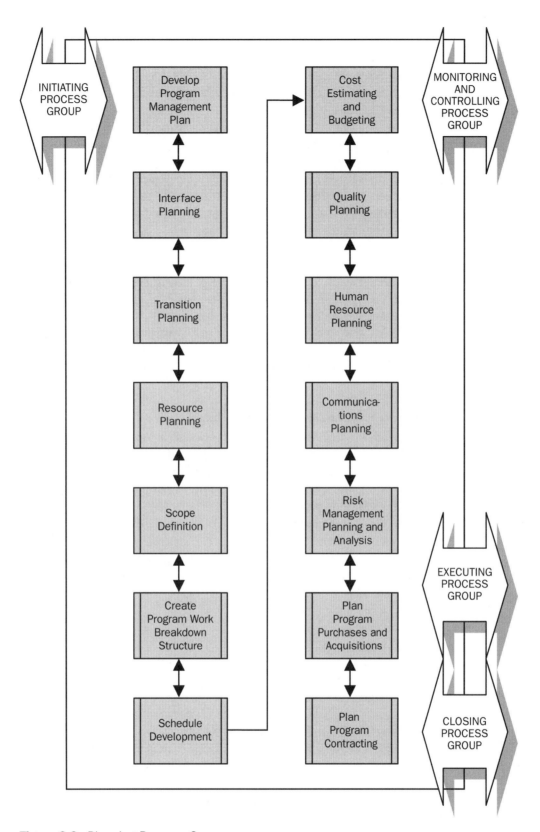

Figure 3-2. Planning Process Group

The Program Planning Processes are iterative and are dependent upon information generated at the project level. During this iterative process, a combination of top-down and bottom-up approaches may be the most suitable. Re-planning is also required at points in the program's performance when scope changes or other unplanned circumstances dictate the need.

Interactions among the processes within the Planning Process Group can vary based on the nature and complexity of the program. The activities of the Planning Process Group include interaction with the portfolio domain.

Planning is performed in the early phase of a program. However, because of both the extended length and the multi-project nature of programs, there are additional milestones where plans should be revisited and updated to ensure ongoing usefulness. These milestones include, but are not limited to:

- New project initiation
- Project closure
- Organization's fiscal year and the budget planning cycle for the program
- Unplanned events that should trigger a review of plans, such as acquisitions and mergers and other major organizational changes
- The output of either the Risk Monitoring and Control Process or the Issue Management and Control Process, when an event sufficiently affects the program, rendering current plans inadequate or ineffective.

3.5.1 Develop Program Management Plan

Develop Program Management Plan is the process of consolidating the outputs of the other Planning Processes, including strategic planning, to create a consistent, coherent set of documents that can be used to guide both program execution and program control. This set of plans includes the following subsidiary plans:

- Benefits management plan
- Communications management plan
- Cost management plan
- Contracts management plan
- Interface management plan
- Scope management plan
- Procurement management plan
- Quality management plan
- Resource management plan
- Risk response plan
- Schedule management plan
- Staffing management plan.

Develop Program Management Plan is an iterative process (along with all of the other Planning Processes), as competing priorities, assumptions, and constraints are worked and resolved to address critical factors, such as business goals, deliverables, benefits, time, and cost.

Each of the other Planning Processes in the program Planning Process Group produces, at a minimum, a plan addressing a specific aspect of the program, such as communications or risks, and a set of supporting documents and detail. These other plans may be incorporated into the program management plan or they may serve as subsidiary plans to the program management plan.

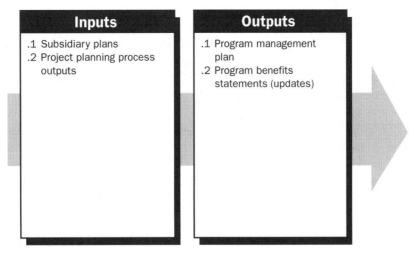

Inputs

.1 Subsidiary plans
.2 Project planning process
   outputs

Outputs

.1 Program management
   plan
.2 Program benefits
   statements (updates)

Table 3-4. Develop Program Management Plan: Inputs and Outputs

3.5.2 Interface Planning

Interface Planning is the process of identifying and mapping interrelationships that exist within a program with other programs in active portfolios or with factors outside the program. It involves describing the characteristics of these interfaces and creating the plan to ensure that these interfaces are established and maintained.

Often, representatives from all involved organizations comprise an integrated program team. Both internal and external interfaces must be addressed. Primarily, interface plans will identify interdependencies; however, they will also support the program communications plan to set up formal communications channels and decision-making relationships.

Whereas the staffing management plan must support the required interfaces in an efficient manner, the interface management plan must take into account existing organizational structures. The risks involved with these interrelationships need to be identified during all phases of program management. This process is typically executed in conjunction with the Human Resource Planning and Communications Planning Processes.

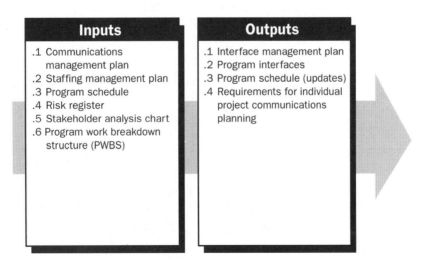

Inputs

.1 Communications
   management plan
.2 Staffing management plan
.3 Program schedule
.4 Risk register
.5 Stakeholder analysis chart
.6 Program work breakdown
   structure (PWBS)

Outputs

.1 Interface management plan
.2 Program interfaces
.3 Program schedule (updates)
.4 Requirements for individual
   project communications
   planning

Table 3-5. Interface Planning: Inputs and Outputs

3.5.3 Transition Planning

Transition Planning is the process of identifying and planning for transitions from the program team to the recipients of on-going activities that result from the program. Typically, transitions are a formal handoff of control of the product, service or benefit/result produced by the program. The purpose of Transition Planning is to ensure that program benefits are sustained once they are transferred to the organization.

Delivered with the transition are all pertinent documents, training and materials, and supporting systems, facilities, and personnel. Transition Planning ensures that the scope of the transition is defined, the stakeholders in the receiving organizations or functions are identified to participate in the planning, the program benefits are measured and sustainment plans exist, and the transition itself is eventually executed. Transition Planning must acknowledge that, within the life of the program, there may be multiple transition events as individual projects close, as interdependent projects close, or as other work activity within the program closes.

The receiver in the transition process will vary depending on the event and on the program type. A product support organization could be the receiver for a product line that a company develops. For a service provided to customers, it could be the service management organization. If the work products are developed for an external customer, the transition could be to the customer's organization. In some cases, the transition may be from one program to another.

Transitions are often formal contract-based activities, but they can also be activities between functions in a single organization. The key to an effective transition plan is a clear understanding of what is to be handed off and the requirements made of the recipient in accepting the handoff.

Program management processes must be complemented by similar processes within the receiving organization. In other words, Transition Planning and the activities within the program are only one part of the complete transition process. The receiving organization or function is responsible for all preparation processes and activities within their domain to ensure that the product, service or result is received and incorporated into their domain.

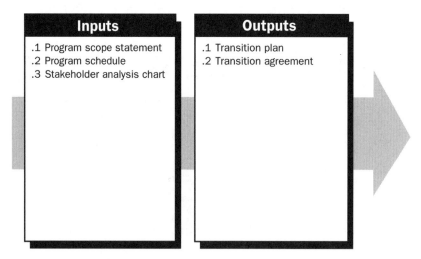

Table 3-6. Transition Planning: Inputs and Outputs

3.5.4 Resource Planning

Resource Planning is the process of determining the people, equipment, materials and other resources that are needed, and in what quantities, in order to perform program activities and optimize the use of available resources across the program. Priority should be given to those skills that are critical to the program but are not possessed by any current program team member. Operational teams and subject matter experts should be actively involved in identifying candidates for the open positions.

Resource Planning at the program level must pay careful attention to how common program resources are allocated across projects to ensure that they are not overcommitted. Historical information regarding what types of resources were required for similar projects on previous programs should be used if available.

Contracts awarded by organizations external to the program can be issued by the customer or sponsor. The product requirements, boundaries of the program, methods of acceptance, and high-level scope statement may be documented in the form of a contract, statement of work (SOW), or program scope statement.

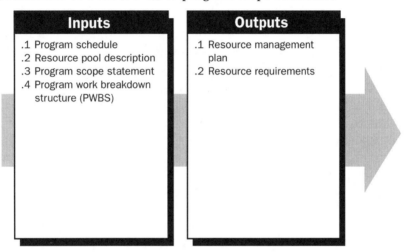

Table 3-7. Resource Planning: Inputs and Outputs

3.5.5 Scope Definition

The Scope Definition Process starts with the program charter, the preliminary scope statement, and benefits realization plan. The objective of this process is to develop a detailed program scope statement. The appropriate approach for deriving the program work breakdown structure (PWBS) (in Section 3.5.6) will also be defined here.

The primary outputs of this process are the program scope statement and scope management plan. The program scope statement becomes the basis for future program decisions and articulates the scope boundaries of the program. The scope management plan identifies how the scope will be managed throughout the program.

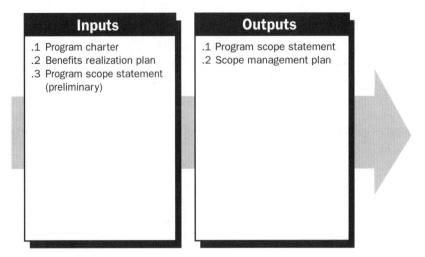

Inputs	Outputs
.1 Program charter .2 Benefits realization plan .3 Program scope statement (preliminary)	.1 Program scope statement .2 Scope management plan

Table 3-8. Scope Definition: Inputs and Outputs

3.5.6 Create Program WBS

The Create Program WBS Process produces a program work breakdown structure (PWBS) that communicates from the program-level perspective a clear understanding and statement of the technical objectives and the end item(s) or end product(s), service(s), or result(s) of the work to be performed.

A PWBS is a deliverable-oriented hierarchical decomposition encompassing the total scope of the program, and includes the deliverables to be produced by the constituent components. Elements not in the PWBS are outside the scope of the program. The PWBS includes, but is not limited to, program management artifacts such as plans, procedures, standards and processes, the major milestones for the program, program management deliverables, and program office support deliverables.

The PWBS is a key to effective control and communication between the program manager and the managers of component projects: the PWBS provides an overview of the program and shows how each project fits in. The decomposition should stop at the level of control required by the program manager. Typically, this will correspond to the first one or two levels of the WBS of each component project. In this way, the PWBS serves as the controlling framework for developing the program schedule, and defines the program manager's management control points that will be used for earned value management, as well as other purposes.

The PWBS components at the lowest level of the PWBS are known as program packages. The complete description of the PWBS components and any additional relevant information is documented in the PWBS dictionary, which is an integral part of the PWBS.

The PWBS does not replace the WBS required of each project within the program. Instead, it is used to clarify the scope of the program, help identify logical groupings of work for components, identify the interface with operations or products, and clarify the program's conclusion. It is also the place to capture all non-project work within the program. This includes program management artifacts developed for use within the program office, external deliverables such as public communications, and end-solution deliverables overarching the projects, such as facilities and infrastructure upgrades.

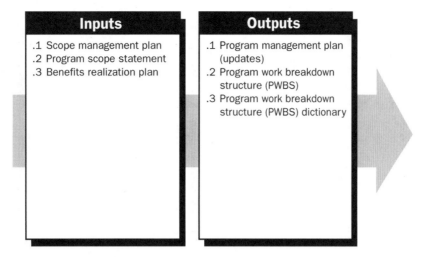

Inputs	Outputs
.1 Scope management plan .2 Program scope statement .3 Benefits realization plan	.1 Program management plan (updates) .2 Program work breakdown structure (PWBS) .3 Program work breakdown structure (PWBS) dictionary

Table 3-9. Create Program WBS: Inputs and Outputs

3.5.7 Schedule Development

Schedule Development is the process of defining the program components needed to produce the program deliverables, determining the order in which the components should be executed, estimating the amount of time required to accomplish each one, identifying significant milestones during the performance period of the program, and documenting the outcome.

A program schedule is typically created using the program work breakdown structure (PWBS) as the starting point. The individual project managers build the detail for their specific project; this detail is rolled up at the management control points into program packages for the PWBS. The interdependencies between the constituent projects must also be reflected and managed in the program schedule. The schedule includes all of the program packages in the PWBS that produce the deliverables. The program schedule will include timelines of various program packages and non-project program activities, and indicate significant milestones.

An essential element of schedule development is determining timing of the program packages, which allows the scheduler to forecast the date on which the program will finish, as well as finish dates for the milestones within the program (e.g., key deliverables within each constituent project).

In addition to producing the program schedule, this process normally creates a plan by which the schedule will be managed over the life of the program. This schedule management plan becomes part of the program management plan.

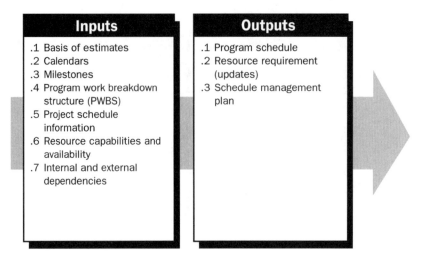

Inputs

.1 Basis of estimates
.2 Calendars
.3 Milestones
.4 Program work breakdown
   structure (PWBS)
.5 Project schedule
   information
.6 Resource capabilities and
   availability
.7 Internal and external
   dependencies

Outputs

.1 Program schedule
.2 Resource requirement
   (updates)
.3 Schedule management
   plan

Table 3-10. Schedule Development: Inputs and Outputs

3.5.8 Cost Estimating and Budgeting

Cost Estimating is the process of aggregating all costs at the program level into a program estimate. It will include all program activity and project and non-project activity. The estimates are either made by the program team for the entire program or aggregated based on individual estimates of projects and work packages.

Cost Budgeting is the process of establishing budgets for the program based on the budgets for the individual projects, the non-project activity and any financial constraints that impose boundaries on the budget. The latter may be a consequence of fiscal year budgetary planning cycles or funding limits for particular periods. Since programs can span multiple planning periods, the program team may use different budget techniques over the program life cycle.

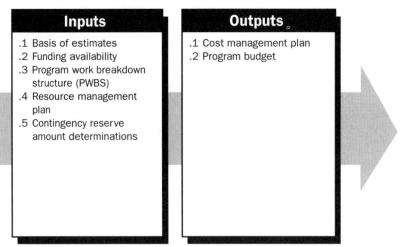

Inputs

.1 Basis of estimates
.2 Funding availability
.3 Program work breakdown
   structure (PWBS)
.4 Resource management
   plan
.5 Contingency reserve
   amount determinations

Outputs

.1 Cost management plan
.2 Program budget

Table 3-11. Cost Estimating and Budgeting: Inputs and Outputs

3.5.9 Quality Planning

Quality Planning is the process of identifying the standards that are relevant to the program and specifying how to satisfy them. Quality Planning and preparation must happen early in the program to ensure that the competency is available during the planning stages of critical program activities and processes. Quality Planning should take advantage of existing quality expertise and methodologies (ISO 9000, Six Sigma, etc.) within the program domain. If the latter are required but do not exist, then they should be implemented within the program.

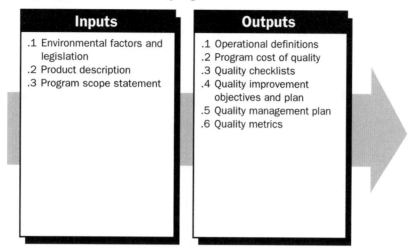

Inputs	Outputs
.1 Environmental factors and legislation .2 Product description .3 Program scope statement	.1 Operational definitions .2 Program cost of quality .3 Quality checklists .4 Quality improvement objectives and plan .5 Quality management plan .6 Quality metrics

Table 3-12. Quality Planning: Inputs and Outputs

3.5.10 Human Resource Planning

Human Resource Planning is the process of identifying, documenting, and assigning program roles, responsibilities, and reporting relationships. The individuals and groups may be part of the program's organization or external to it. Internal organizational elements include the program management team, representatives from functional areas within the enterprise, such as finance and human resources, and key individuals in the project management teams that are under the jurisdiction of the program manager. External organizational entities may include external end-users of the solution(s) delivered by the program, as well as other organizations with a stake in the program and its successful outcome.

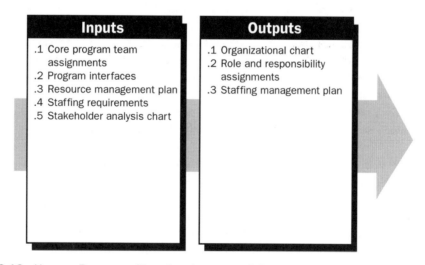

Inputs	Outputs
.1 Core program team assignments .2 Program interfaces .3 Resource management plan .4 Staffing requirements .5 Stakeholder analysis chart	.1 Organizational chart .2 Role and responsibility assignments .3 Staffing management plan

Table 3-13. Human Resource Planning: Inputs and Outputs

3.5.11 Communications Planning

Communications Planning is the process of determining the information and communication needs of the program stakeholders, who needs what information, when they need it, how it will be given to them and by whom.

Adequate communications requirements must be conveyed as input to the projects in order to facilitate information capture from the projects to be fed back into the program.

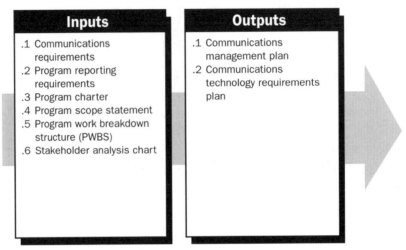

Inputs	Outputs
.1 Communications requirements .2 Program reporting requirements .3 Program charter .4 Program scope statement .5 Program work breakdown structure (PWBS) .6 Stakeholder analysis chart	.1 Communications management plan .2 Communications technology requirements plan

Table 3-14. Communications Planning: Inputs and Outputs

3.5.12 Risk Management Planning and Analysis

Risk Management Planning and Analysis is the process of deciding how to plan and analyze risk management activities for a program, including risks identified in the individual program components.

Risk Management Planning and Analysis consists of four steps:
- Identification of the risks affecting the program and documenting their characteristics on a regular basis throughout the program
- Qualitative risk analysis of the effects of risks and conditions on the delivery of program benefits
- Quantitative risk analysis of the probability and consequences of risks, and evaluating their implications for program benefits delivery, in order to prioritize risk responses
- Risk response planning to develop procedures and techniques to enhance opportunities and reduce threats to the delivery of program benefits.

It is important that the program management involvement in risk should support the risk management activities of the program components. Program-specific risk activities include the following:
- Identifying and analyzing inter-project risks;
- Reviewing the risk response plans of the program components for proposed actions that could affect other components and modifying them as needed
- Determining root causes
- Proposing solutions to risks escalated by component managers

- Implementing response mechanisms that benefit more than one component
- Managing a contingency reserve (in terms of cost and/or time) consolidated across the entire program.

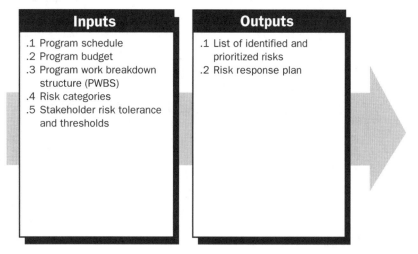

Inputs	Outputs
.1 Program schedule .2 Program budget .3 Program work breakdown structure (PWBS) .4 Risk categories .5 Stakeholder risk tolerance and thresholds	.1 List of identified and prioritized risks .2 Risk response plan

Table 3-15. Risk Management Planning and Analysis: Inputs and Outputs

3.5.13 Plan Program Purchases and Acquisitions

Plan Program Purchases and Acquisitions is the process of determining what to procure and when, validating product requirements, and developing procurement strategies. This process precedes the Plan Program Contracting Process and generates several outputs that become inputs to contract planning.

A primary function of Plan Program Purchases and Acquisitions is to analyze the program scope statement, the product descriptions that define the deliverables, and the program work breakdown structure (PWBS). Make-or-buy decision techniques are applied to the results of the analyses to determine which PWBS elements will be produced using internal resources available to the program and which will be obtained from outside suppliers. Once these determinations are made and approved, this information is passed to the Plan Program Contracting Process, where potential sources are identified and formal contracting documents are created.

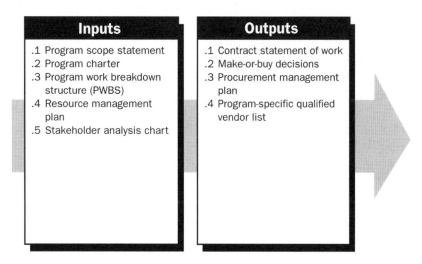

Inputs	Outputs
.1 Program scope statement .2 Program charter .3 Program work breakdown structure (PWBS) .4 Resource management plan .5 Stakeholder analysis chart	.1 Contract statement of work .2 Make-or-buy decisions .3 Procurement management plan .4 Program-specific qualified vendor list

Table 3-16. Plan Program Purchases and Acquisitions: Inputs and Outputs

3.5.14 Plan Program Contracting

Plan Program Contracting is the process of identifying the type and detail of documentation required to implement contracts for suppliers either external to or within the organization. For a program, the range and complexity of documentation for contracting will be far greater than for a project. For example, most often contracting at the program level needs to address legal issues and considerations. This process produces the foundation and guidelines on which an effective program-level contract administration process can be implemented.

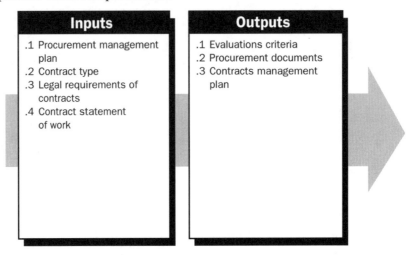

Inputs	Outputs
.1 Procurement management plan .2 Contract type .3 Legal requirements of contracts .4 Contract statement of work	.1 Evaluations criteria .2 Procurement documents .3 Contracts management plan

Table 3-17. Plan Program Contracting: Inputs and Outputs

3.6 Executing Process Group

The Executing Process Group is comprised of the processes that drive the program work in accordance with the program management plan and its subsidiary plans, if applicable. These processes ensure that benefits management, stakeholder management, and program governance are executed in accordance with established policies and plans.

Using these processes, the program team acquires and marshals the resources needed to accomplish the goals and benefits of the program, including internal program staff, contractors, and suppliers.

The Executing Process Group involves managing the cost, quality, and schedule plans, often as an integrated plan, and providing status information and requested changes to the program's Monitoring and Controlling Process Group, through approved change requests, corrective actions, and preventive actions.

The Executing Process Group also ensures that all stakeholders receive necessary information in a timely manner. This includes administering all of the program's communications channels and providing information such as status updates, notifications of change requests and approvals, and responses to governmental and regulatory agencies.

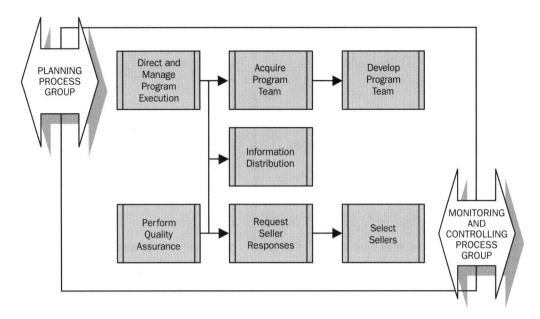

Figure 3-3. Executing Process Group

3.6.1 Direct and Manage Program Execution

Direct and Manage Program Execution is the process of delivering the program's intended benefits. This process focuses specifically on those projects and program work packages currently in progress and integrates other Executing Processes. Its purpose is to produce the cumulative deliverables and other work products of the program. It facilitates and resolves inter-project issues, risks, and constraints.

Program management plan execution becomes the primary responsibility of the program manager and the program team once the initial planning activities are completed and execution of the program has begun (although the other Process Groups remain active, particularly Planning and Monitoring and Controlling). Progress of the work is tracked regularly via updates on individual projects, and is passed on to the Performance Reporting Process.

In addition to producing deliverables, this process implements approved change requests, corrective actions, and preventive actions once they have been integrated with the relevant plans. Finally, this process is responsible for ensuring that all transition plans are executed at both the project and program level.

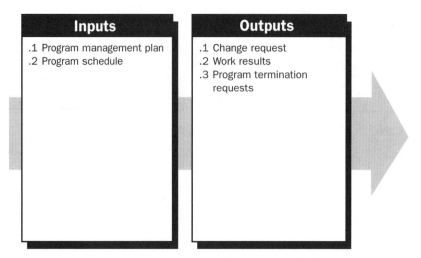

Inputs	Outputs
.1 Program management plan .2 Program schedule	.1 Change request .2 Work results .3 Program termination requests

Table 3-18. Direct and Manage Program Execution: Inputs and Outputs

3.6.2 Perform Quality Assurance

Perform Quality Assurance is the process of evaluating overall program performance on a regular basis to provide confidence that the program will comply with the relevant quality policies and standards. It is performed throughout the life cycle of the program.

The Perform Quality Assurance Process, within and of a program, is not intended to replace component quality assurance efforts. Rather, Perform Quality Assurance focuses on cross-program, inter-project and non-project activities, including the service management activities of the program and the overarching quality needs of the customer.

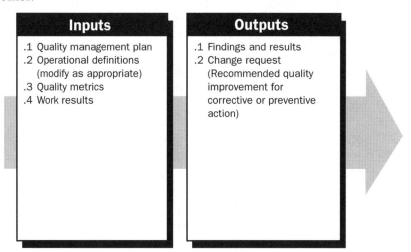

Inputs	Outputs
.1 Quality management plan .2 Operational definitions (modify as appropriate) .3 Quality metrics .4 Work results	.1 Findings and results .2 Change request (Recommended quality improvement for corrective or preventive action)

Table 3-19. Perform Quality Assurance: Inputs and Outputs

3.6.3 Acquire Program Team

The Acquire Program Team Process addresses the provision of human resources for the program through selection of internal or external candidates. The decision to use internal versus external resources depends upon several factors. These include the length of time that a particular skill set is needed, the availability of internal resources with the right skill sets, the cost of external resources, and the timing of the need.

Staffing internally involves identifying existing personnel qualified for open positions, negotiating for their services with their current management, and then transitioning them to the program position. Negotiations involve the tradeoffs encountered when moving someone from an existing position, with its corresponding responsibilities and deliverables, to the program role in the most effective manner. Consideration must be given to the needs of existing assignments, the person's fit for the position, the person's career path, and his or her ability to fit into the program environment.

Staffing externally involves the process of identifying and evaluating external candidates and then selecting the best candidate for the position. Staffing externally can mean hiring a full-time employee or securing services on a contract or consulting basis. Consideration must be given to the long-term value of the hired skill to the organization, and whether intellectual property acquired by the person would be better retained in the organization by full-time employment. Another consideration is the cost of recruiting and hiring external candidates as employees versus subcontracting, retaining consulting staff, or rescheduling activities based on the availability of internal staff.

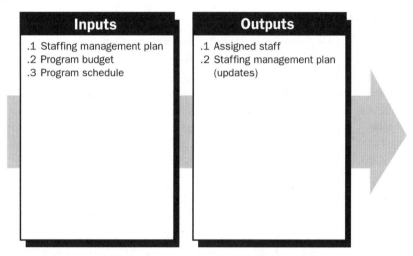

Table 3-20. Acquire Program Team: Inputs and Outputs

3.6.4 Develop Program Team

Develop Program Team is the process of building individual and group competencies to enhance program performance. Typically, these are competencies specifically needed on the program team for the effective performance of the program. A successful development plan will balance the needs of the program with the needs of the individual's career path.

Develop Program Team is an ongoing process throughout the program. In addition to developing personnel for current assignments and roles, personnel development needs to address succession planning, preparing individuals to assume different or larger roles within the program at some future date, and reassignment of personnel as the program concludes.

The process will support development of personnel by providing necessary knowledge and skills particular to the program or to relevant program management competencies.

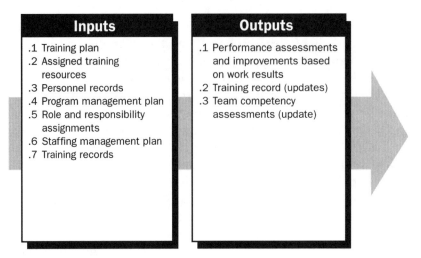

Inputs	Outputs
.1 Training plan .2 Assigned training resources .3 Personnel records .4 Program management plan .5 Role and responsibility assignments .6 Staffing management plan .7 Training records	.1 Performance assessments and improvements based on work results .2 Training record (updates) .3 Team competency assessments (update)

Table 3-21. Develop Program Team: Inputs and Outputs

3.6.5 Information Distribution

Information Distribution is the process of providing timely and accurate information to program stakeholders in useful formats and appropriate media. It includes administration of three major communications channels: the clients, the sponsors, and the component managers. Distributed information can include the following:

- Status information on the program and projects, including progress, cost information, risk analysis, and other relevant information to internal or external audiences
- Notification of change requests to the program and project teams, and eventually notification of the response to the change requests
- Internal budgetary information
- External filings with government and regulatory bodies as prescribed by laws and regulations
- Public announcements communicating information useful to the general public.

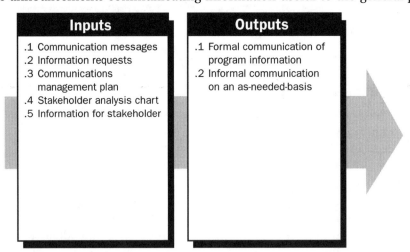

Inputs	Outputs
.1 Communication messages .2 Information requests .3 Communications management plan .4 Stakeholder analysis chart .5 Information for stakeholder	.1 Formal communication of program information .2 Informal communication on an as-needed-basis

Table 3-22. Information Distribution: Inputs and Outputs

3.6.6 Request Seller Responses

Request Seller Responses is the process of issuing requests for information (RFI), requests for proposal (RFP), and requests for quotation (RFQ), and obtaining the responses. These formal documents (RFI, RFP, RFQ) are used in the early stages of planning to help evaluate "make versus buy" decisions, as well as to gain an understanding of seller interest and qualifications.

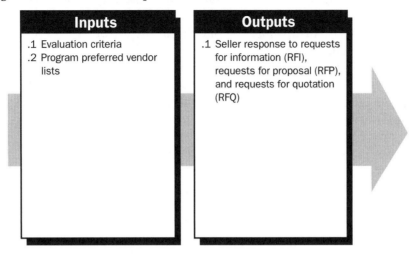

Table 3-23. Request Seller Responses: Inputs and Outputs

3.6.7 Select Sellers

Select Sellers is the process for reviewing offers, choosing among potential sellers, and negotiating the details of the contract, including technical terms and conditions, roles and responsibilities, deliverables, and final cost. The program-level responsibility is to negotiate and finalize program-wide policies and agreements such as basic order agreements and integrated volume discounts. The activity of completing the contract between sellers and customer formally and legally is the responsibility of the Program Contract Administration Process.

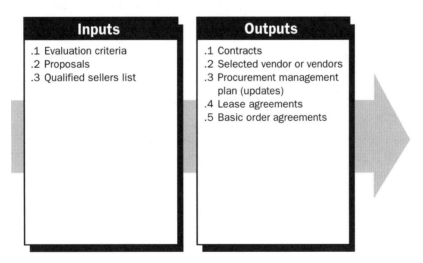

Table 3-24. Select Sellers: Inputs and Outputs

3.7 Monitoring and Controlling Process Group

At the program level, monitoring and controlling involves obtaining and consolidating data on status and progress from individual projects or program packages (i.e., non-project tasks). Monitoring also entails interfacing with the program governance structure to ensure the organization has a clear picture of the current benefit delivery and expected future benefits.

Effective program performance reporting supports appropriate preventive and corrective actions at the program level, especially during the delivering benefits phase of the program life cycle. In addition, these corrective actions could also be a result of governance oversight, especially when programs require statutory compliance with external and governmental agencies.

For programs, integrated change control involves redirecting or modifying the program as needed, based on feedback from individual projects or work packages. In addition, changes could originate from interfaces with other subsystems of the program or factors external to the program. The latter could be due to government regulations, market changes, the economy, or political issues.

3.7.1 Integrated Change Control

Integrated Change Control is the process of coordinating changes across the entire program, including changes to cost, quality, schedule, and scope. This process controls the approval and refusal of requests for change, escalates requests in line with authority thresholds, determines when changes have occurred, influences factors that create changes, makes sure those changes are beneficial and agreed-upon, and manages how and when the approved changes are applied. Analysis of the change request involves identifying, documenting, and estimating all of the work that the change would entail, including a list of all of the program management processes that need to be carried out again (such as updating the program work breakdown structure (PWBS), revising the program risk register, etc.). Integrated Change Control is performed throughout the entire program life cycle from initiation through closure.

Inputs for this process include change requests from components and from program-level and non-project activities. The outputs from this process feed back to the component level and, as such, the process is iterative between the program and component domains.

3.7.2 Resource Control

Resource Control is the process of managing all program resources, and their associated cost, according to the program management plan.

Resource Control is the process of monitoring human resources to ensure that committed resources are made available to the program consistent with commitments, resources are allocated within the program according to the plan, and resources are released from the program as dictated by the plan. Resource Control may include authorized cross-charging or other forms of allocation of expenses between the program, component, and contributing functions within the organization.

Other resources include plants, test beds, laboratories, data centers, office space, and other facilities, including real estate leases or purchases, equipment of all types, software, vehicles, and office supplies. Some resources, such as office supplies, are consumed by the program and must be managed as an expense.

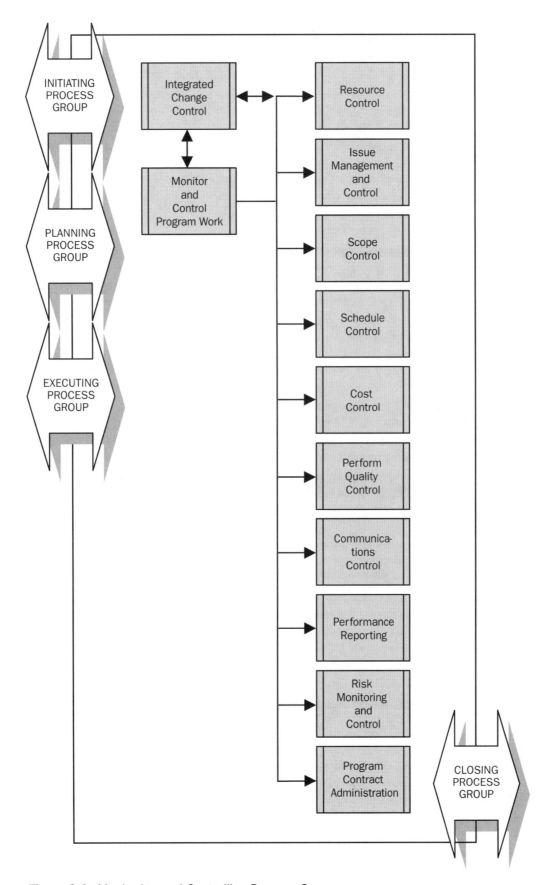

Figure 3-4. Monitoring and Controlling Process Group

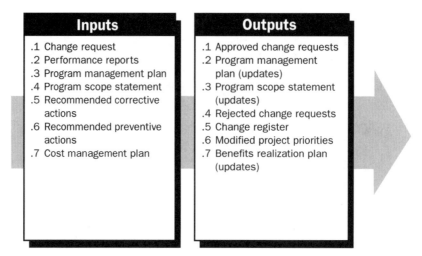

Inputs	Outputs
.1 Change request	.1 Approved change requests
.2 Performance reports	.2 Program management plan (updates)
.3 Program management plan	.3 Program scope statement (updates)
.4 Program scope statement	.4 Rejected change requests
.5 Recommended corrective actions	.5 Change register
.6 Recommended preventive actions	.6 Modified project priorities
.7 Cost management plan	.7 Benefits realization plan (updates)

Table 3-25. Integrated Change Control: Inputs and Outputs

Purchased non-consumable resources must be tracked to ensure that they are returned for other use or made available for sale when they are no longer needed for the purposes of the program, and to allow accurate financial tracking and reporting. Some resources (e.g., software programs, office equipment) are transferred to the receiving entity when the program is transitioned. Leased resources must be tracked to ensure that they are returned at the expiration of the lease or when they are no longer required, to avoid penalties or the hidden expense of ongoing lease payments.

Finally, Resource Control includes analysis of resource expenses assigned to the program to ensure correctness and completeness.

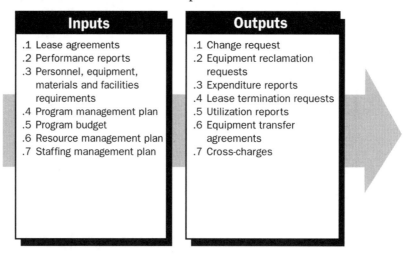

Inputs	Outputs
.1 Lease agreements	.1 Change request
.2 Performance reports	.2 Equipment reclamation requests
.3 Personnel, equipment, materials and facilities requirements	.3 Expenditure reports
.4 Program management plan	.4 Lease termination requests
.5 Program budget	.5 Utilization reports
.6 Resource management plan	.6 Equipment transfer agreements
.7 Staffing management plan	.7 Cross-charges

Table 3-26. Resource Control: Inputs and Outputs

3.7.3 Monitor and Control Program Work

Monitor and Control Program Work is the process of collecting, measuring and consolidating performance information, and assessing measurements and trends to generate improvements. The Monitor and Control Program Work Process focuses on individual project reporting to understand each project's performance as it relates to the overall program, as well as reporting on non-project deliverables being produced at the program level.

These reported project results, plus those from the non-project activities, are analyzed, focusing on their interrelationships to identify conflicts and adverse impacts that must be corrected, to identify opportunities that can be leveraged, and to determine which of these factors should result in modification of the program management plan. This is similar to risk management; however, it is focused on performance as opposed to risks. The consolidated information can be made available to stakeholders through the Information Distribution Process.

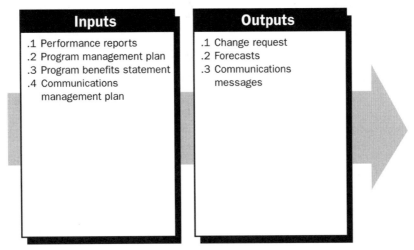

Table 3-27. Monitor and Control Program Work: Inputs and Outputs

3.7.4 Issue Management and Control

Issue Management and Control is the process of identifying, tracking, and closing issues effectively to ensure that stakeholder expectations are aligned with program activities and deliverables. This alignment can be accomplished by several approaches, including modification of requirements or the program scope, adjusting organizational policies, or changing stakeholder expectations.

Issue Management and Control at the program level can also include addressing the issues escalated from the constituent projects that could not be resolved at the project level. These unresolved project issues can impact the overall progress of the program and must be tracked.

When an issue is identified, it is recorded in an issues register and subjected to analysis by a reviewing authority or body. Issue reviews should be conducted on a regular schedule to track the status of all open issues. It is essential that each issue be associated with an owner who has the authority and means to resolve and close the issue; when an issue is unresolved, it is then escalated progressively higher on the authority scale until resolution can be achieved. There should be a governance process and procedures that selectively allow issues to receive appropriate visibility for possible impact across other portfolios within the organization.

The Issue Management and Control Process is carried out in parallel with controlling risk, especially those risks which do not get resolved at the project level.

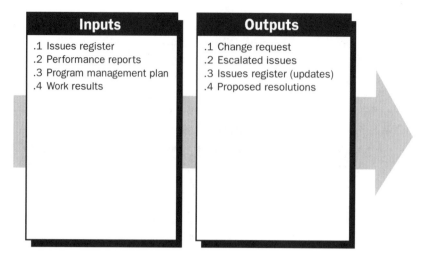

Inputs	Outputs
.1 Issues register	.1 Change request
.2 Performance reports	.2 Escalated issues
.3 Program management plan	.3 Issues register (updates)
.4 Work results	.4 Proposed resolutions

Table 3-28. Issue Management and Control: Inputs and Outputs

3.7.5 Scope Control

Scope Control is the process for controlling changes to the program scope. This is a formal process for accomplishing the following tasks:
- Capturing requested changes
- Evaluating each requested change
- Deciding the disposition of each requested change
- Communicating a decision to impacted stakeholders
- Archiving the change request and its supporting detail
- When a request is accepted, initiating the activities required to have the change incorporated into the program management plan.

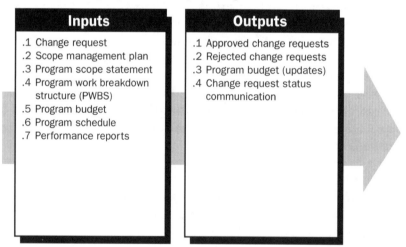

Inputs	Outputs
.1 Change request	.1 Approved change requests
.2 Scope management plan	.2 Rejected change requests
.3 Program scope statement	.3 Program budget (updates)
.4 Program work breakdown structure (PWBS)	.4 Change request status communication
.5 Program budget	
.6 Program schedule	
.7 Performance reports	

Table 3-29. Scope Control: Inputs and Outputs

3.7.6 Schedule Control

Schedule Control is the process of ensuring that the program will produce its required deliverables and solutions on time. The activities in this process include tracking the actual start and finish of activities and milestones against the planned timeline, and updating the plan so that the comparison to the plan is always current. Schedule

Control must work closely with the other program and portfolio control processes. It involves identifying not only slippages, but also opportunities.

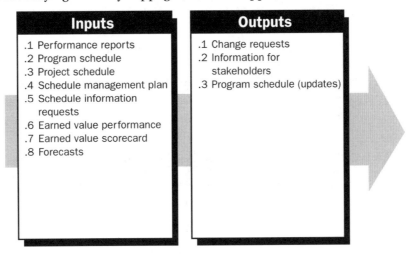

Inputs

.1 Performance reports
.2 Program schedule
.3 Project schedule
.4 Schedule management plan
.5 Schedule information requests
.6 Earned value performance
.7 Earned value scorecard
.8 Forecasts

Outputs

.1 Change requests
.2 Information for stakeholders
.3 Program schedule (updates)

Table 3-30. Schedule Control: Inputs and Outputs

3.7.7 Cost Control

Cost Control is the process of controlling changes to, and producing information from, the program budget. Cost Control is proactive, analyzing actual cost as incurred against the plan to identify variance from the plan, and, where possible, doing trend analysis to predict problem areas early. Cost Control is also reactive, dealing with unanticipated events or necessary but unplanned activities that affect the budget either negatively or positively. Cost Control is frequently thought of as merely holding down cost so that the program remains on budget, or bringing it back to budget when there is an overrun. However, of equal importance, cost control involves identifying opportunities to return funding from the program to the enterprise wherever possible.

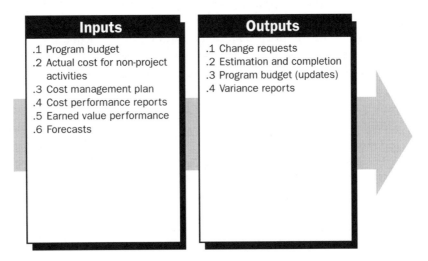

Inputs

.1 Program budget
.2 Actual cost for non-project activities
.3 Cost management plan
.4 Cost performance reports
.5 Earned value performance
.6 Forecasts

Outputs

.1 Change requests
.2 Estimation and completion
.3 Program budget (updates)
.4 Variance reports

Table 3-31. Cost Control: Inputs and Outputs

3.7.8 Perform Quality Control

Perform Quality Control is the process of monitoring specific program deliverables and results to determine if they fulfill quality requirements. This process identifies faulty outcomes and allows the elimination of causes of unsatisfactory performance at all stages of the quality loop, from the identification of needs to the assessment of whether the identified needs have been satisfied or not. The Perform Quality Control Process ensures that quality plans are executed at project levels, via quality reviews and project management health checks. Perform Quality Control is performed throughout the program. Program results include both products and services, such as deliverables, management results, and cost and schedule performance.

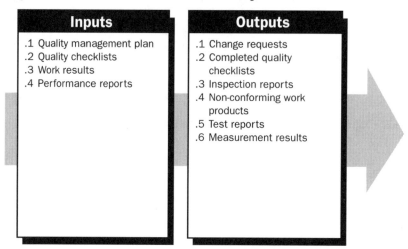

Inputs	Outputs
.1 Quality management plan .2 Quality checklists .3 Work results .4 Performance reports	.1 Change requests .2 Completed quality checklists .3 Inspection reports .4 Non-conforming work products .5 Test reports .6 Measurement results

Table 3-32. Perform Quality Control: Inputs and Outputs

3.7.9 Communications Control

Communications Control is the process of managing communications to inform the stakeholders about the program and resolve issues of interest to them. The Communications Control Process ensures that policies and procedures are received, recorded, and routed to the intended recipients (through the Information Distribution Process). The scope and extent of this process is much wider at the program level than at the project level. Apart from the program sponsor, the other stakeholders involved in a program could include product managers, financial managers, and senior management personnel, especially those involved in strategic planning.

Furthermore, since programs tend to be of larger size, greater cost, and much longer in duration, proactive communication is required with the community at large. Such external communications will not only include addressing issues specific to a program, such as environmental issues, but also managing public and media relations at the social and political level as may be appropriate to the program.

3.7.10 Performance Reporting

Performance Reporting is the process of consolidating performance data to provide stakeholders with information about how resources are being used to deliver program benefits.

Performance reporting aggregates all performance information across projects and non-project activity to provide a clear picture of the program performance as a whole.

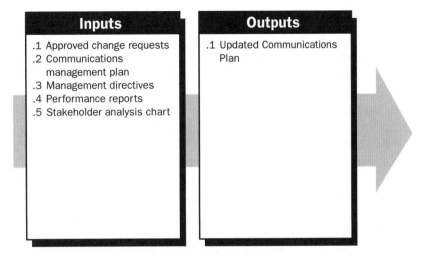

Inputs	Outputs
.1 Approved change requests .2 Communications management plan .3 Management directives .4 Performance reports .5 Stakeholder analysis chart	.1 Updated Communications Plan

Table 3-33. Communications Control: Inputs and Outputs

This information is conveyed to the stakeholders by means of the Information Distribution process to provide them with needed status and deliverable information. Additionally, this information is provided to stakeholders of the program and its constituent projects for the purpose of providing them with general and background information about the program's performance.

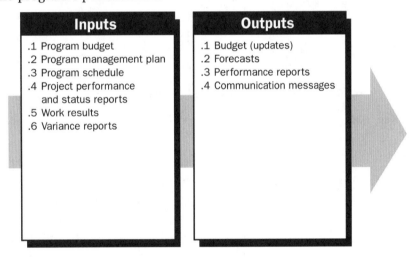

Inputs	Outputs
.1 Program budget .2 Program management plan .3 Program schedule .4 Project performance and status reports .5 Work results .6 Variance reports	.1 Budget (updates) .2 Forecasts .3 Performance reports .4 Communication messages

Table 3-34. Performance Reporting: Inputs and Outputs

3.7.11 Risk Monitoring and Control

Risk Monitoring and Control is the process of tracking identified program risks, identifying new risks to the program, executing risk response plans, and evaluating their effectiveness in reducing risk through the program life cycle. They include oversight of risks and responses at the project level within the program. Risk Monitoring and Control is an ongoing process.

Risk monitoring involves tracking program-level risks currently identified in the risk response plan and identifying new risks that emerge during the execution of the program, for example, unresolved project-level risks that demand resolution at the program level. It includes determining whether new risks have developed, current risks have changed, risks have been triggered, risk responses are in effect where necessary and are effective, and if program assumptions are still valid.

Risk control focuses on risks that threaten to develop into actual problems or have already done so. Risk control involves implementing the response actions and contingency plans contained in the risk response plan.

When risks remain unresolved, the program manager ensures that these risks are escalated progressively higher on the authority scale until resolution can be achieved. Governance process and procedures should be in place to allow risks to be assessed as necessary for possible impact across the organization.

Program risk situations, plans, and the status and the effectiveness of ongoing or completed risk responses should be included in program management reviews. All modifications resulting from reviews and other changes in risks should be entered in the risk response plan.

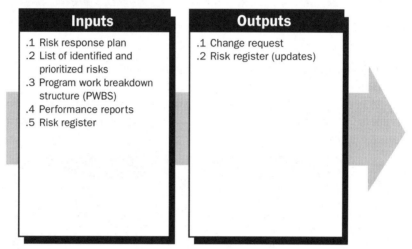

Inputs	Outputs
.1 Risk response plan .2 List of identified and prioritized risks .3 Program work breakdown structure (PWBS) .4 Performance reports .5 Risk register	.1 Change request .2 Risk register (updates)

Table 3-35. Risk Monitoring and Control: Inputs and Outputs

3.7.12 Program Contract Administration

Program contract administration is the process of managing the relationship with sellers and buyers at the program level, excluding such processes performed at the component level. The process includes purchases and procurement of outside resources that span the program domain and that are not covered by a specific project.

The program management team must be aware of the legal, political, and managerial implications during implementation, since contractual issues can affect deadlines, have legal and costly consequences, and can produce adverse publicity. The team must effectively communicate with sponsors, sellers, governing bodies, and the project and program management teams.

At the program level, program contract administration relies on the interaction of other program and project processes.

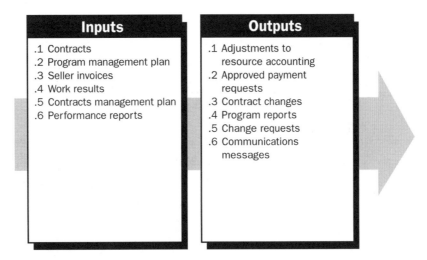

Inputs	Outputs
.1 Contracts .2 Program management plan .3 Seller invoices .4 Work results .5 Contracts management plan .6 Performance reports	.1 Adjustments to resource accounting .2 Approved payment requests .3 Contract changes .4 Program reports .5 Change requests .6 Communications messages

Table 3-36. Program Contract Administration: Inputs and Outputs

3.8 Closing Process Group

The Closing Process Group formalizes acceptance of products, services, or results that bring the program, or a project within a program, to completion. The Closing Process Group includes the processes required to terminate formally all the activities of a program, finalize closure of a project within the program and hand-off the completed product to others, or to close a cancelled program or project within the program.

The purposes of the Closing Processes include the following:

- To demonstrate that all program benefits have been delivered and that the scope of work has been fulfilled or to document the current state in the case of early termination
- To demonstrate that contractual obligations with the seller and/or the customer have been met or to document the current state in the case of early termination
- To demonstrate that all payments to the seller or from the customer have been delivered or to document the current state in the case of early termination
- To release all human resources and to demonstrate that all other resources have either been made available to other activities, sold, discarded, returned to the owner, transferred to the organization maintaining the product or service, or transferred to the customer, or otherwise disposed of
- To demonstrate that all required documentation has been archived in the manner prescribed by the program management plan, or to document the current state in the case of early termination
- To demonstrate that any intellectual property developed during the course of the program has been captured and documented for future use, in a manner that ensures legal protection of this valuable asset
- To transition ongoing activities such as product support, service management, or customer support from a project or the program to an operational support function
- To leave in place a legacy of operational benefit sustainment, deriving optimum value from the work accomplished by the program.

Program closure activities happen throughout the program, not just at program completion. As specific projects and other activities are completed, closing activities must occur. Otherwise, valuable program information will be lost, and there is a potential that the program will not meet its closure obligations.

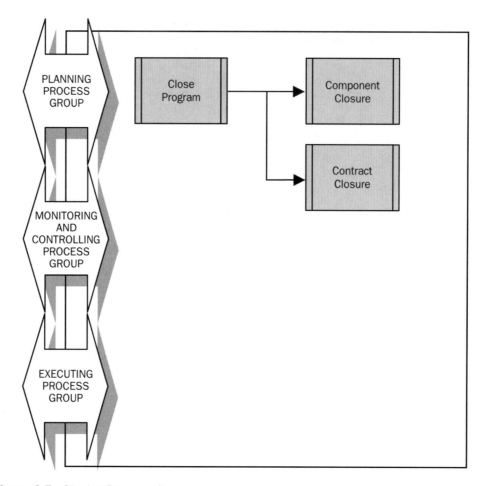

Figure 3-5. Closing Process Group

3.8.1 Close Program

Close Program is the process of formalizing the acceptance of the program's outcome by the sponsor or customer. However, administrative closure should not wait until the program has completed the execution process. Projects under the program need to be closed before the program is closed. As each project or each non-project activity closes, the Close Program Process should be performed to capture information and records, archive them, communicate the closure event and status, and obtain sponsor or customer sign-off.

Formal acceptance of the program is achieved by reviewing, with the sponsor or customer, the program scope and the closure documents of the program's constituent projects and non-project activities. These closure documents include the sponsor's or customer's sign-off of the projects or non-project activities, and the results of any verification of deliverables against requirements. Once the review is complete, the sponsor or customer is asked to acknowledge a final acceptance by signing the closure documents.

During this process, the lessons learned are input from other program management processes that created them as outputs. In this process, they are analyzed, significant lessons learned are incorporated into the closure report output, and all lessons learned are included in the program archives.

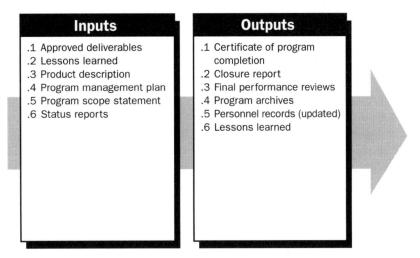

Table 3-37. Close Program: Inputs and Outputs

3.8.2 Component Closure

Component Closure is the process of performing program management activities to close out a project or other non-project activity within the program. Program component closure deals with these closure issues at the program level, that is, it is informed by and performed at a higher level than normal project closure occurring at the project level. This process involves validating and ensuring that the project closure has indeed taken place at the project level. The resources that become available may be reallocated to other components that are either active or awaiting activation within the program. Project records must be closed and archived as needed. Communications to a larger or different set of stakeholders than those at the project level may be needed, as well.

The information required for this process is obtained from each of the projects or work packages. For a program, component closure will normally be done at the end of the project life cycle. However, project closure may need to be done if a project is being terminated before the completion of its life cycle. This can be the result of a program benefits review or changes in the external environment.

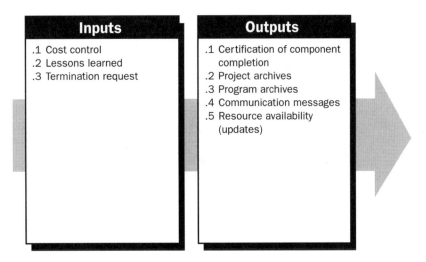

Table 3-38. Component Closure: Inputs and Outputs

3.8.3 Contract Closure

Contract Closure is the process of closing out a contract executed during the program and on behalf of the program, in accordance with the contract's terms and conditions. This process also applies to cases of premature contract termination.

Contract Closure involves both product verification (i.e., verifying that the work was done) and the updating of all contract records. In the case of premature termination, it involves documentation of actual work performed plus work not performed, the circumstances that caused termination, and the updating of all contract records. Contract records are important and include the contract itself and other relevant documentation, such as progress reports, financial records, invoices, and payment records. These are often kept in a contract file, which should be part of the complete program file.

Contract documentation is also important should a procurement audit or legal action be initiated. Such an audit is a structured review of the procurement process from procurement planning through contract administration. In case of legal action, accurate and complete documentation is critical for swift resolution.

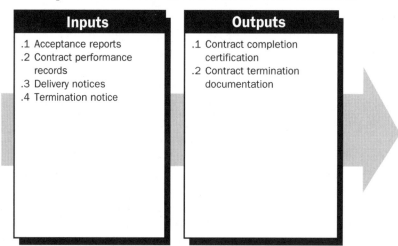

Inputs	Outputs
.1 Acceptance reports .2 Contract performance records .3 Delivery notices .4 Termination notice	.1 Contract completion certification .2 Contract termination documentation

Table 3-39. Contract Closure: Inputs and Outputs

3.9 Process Interactions

There are many interactions among program management processes. Processes receive inputs from processes that logically precede them and send outputs to successor processes. In some cases, an output from a process becomes an input to the same process, for example, when a Planning Process iteratively updates a plan over time.

There are cases where an output of a process may pass through several other processes in succession before returning as an input to its originating process, and more typically, cases where an output from a process travels along a "one-way street." An example of this is lessons learned, produced as output from many processes and flowing to a single closing process, Close Program, to be analyzed, incorporated into a program closure report, and then archived.

The complexity of the program management process model is increased when inputs and outputs flow between the project domain, the program domain and the portfolio domain. This can be illustrated with a few examples:

- Project schedules flow to the program domain as inputs to the Schedule Control Process, in order to update the program's integrated master schedule.
- Project risks flow to the program's Risk Management Planning and Analysis Process in a similar manner to create a comprehensive view of risks to the program.
- Corrective actions may be created by program management processes and flow back to the project domain.
- Funding availability outputs flow from the portfolio domain to the program's Cost Estimating and Budgeting Process as inputs to the program budget, while cost performance reports from the program flow back to the portfolio domain.

3.10 Program Management Process Mapping

As previously discussed, the program management processes defined in this standard are organized into five Program Management Process Groups. The *PMBOK® Guide—Third Edition* defines nine Project Management Knowledge Areas. In the table below, the program management processes are associated with their respective Process Groups and correlated to the nine Knowledge Areas in which most of the activities associated with the program take place.

Project Management Knowledge Areas	Initiating Process Group	Planning Process Group	Executing Process Group	Monitoring and Controlling Process Group	Closing Process Group
Integration Management	Initiate Program Authorize Projects	Develop Program Management Plan • Interface Planning • Transition Planning • Resource Planning	Direct and Manage Program Execution	Integrated Change Control Resource Control Monitor and Control Program Work Issue Management and Control	Close Program Component Closure
Scope Management		Scope Definition Create Program Work Breakdown Structure		Scope Control	
Time Management		Schedule Development		Schedule Control	
Cost Management		Cost Estimating and Budgeting		Cost Control	
Quality Management		Quality Planning	Perform Quality Assurance	Perform Quality Control	
Human Resource Management	Initiate Team	Human Resource Planning	Acquire Program Team Develop Program Team		
Communications Management		Communica-tions Planning	Information Distribution	Communica-tions Control Performance Reporting	
Risk Management		Risk Management Planning and Analysis		Risk Monitoring and Control	
Procurement Management		Plan Program Purchases and Acquisitions Plan Program Contracting	Request Seller Responses Select Sellers	Program Contract Administration	Contract Closure

Table 3-40. Program Management Process Groups and Knowledge Areas Mapping

Section III

Appendices

Appendix A

(Reserved for documenting future updates)

Appendix B

Initial Development of *The Standard for Program Management*

B.1 Introduction

Since 1996, project managers and organizations have recognized the standard for one project: PMI's *A Guide to the Project Management Body of Knowledge* (*PMBOK® Guide*). Then in 2003, PMI introduced its first standard for organizations called the *Organizational Project Management Maturity Model* (*OPM3®*).

Early in 2003, recognizing that the project management profession encompasses a much broader field, including managing multiple projects through programs and portfolios, PMI's Standards Program Team (SPT—which includes the PMI Manager of Standards plus the Member Advisory Group) chartered the development of "a standard, or standards," for program management and portfolio management processes.

Like the *PMBOK® Guide* standard for "most projects most of the time," the charter for the PPMS (Program and Portfolio Management Standards) Program was to focus on processes that are generally recognized as good practice most of the time. Moreover, the new standard or standards were to emulate the *PMBOK® Guide*—Third Edition, specifically excluding Knowledge Areas as well as tools and techniques. The new standard or standards, however, were to map content relationships to processes and Knowledge Areas lined in the *PMBOK® Guide*—Third Edition.

B.2 Preliminary Work

In the summer of 2003, the PPMS Team formed, eventually including 416 PMI volunteers representing 36 countries under the leadership of David Ross, Project Manager, and Paul Shaltry, Deputy Project Manager.

One of the first challenges was the need to establish common agreement on the key definitions, in this case, "program," "program management," "portfolio," and "portfolio management." The PMI Standards Manager brought together all of the active standards teams to achieve consensus on these definitions. The involved team leaders agreed in time for common definitions to be included in the *PMBOK® Guide—Third Edition* and form the foundation for the program and portfolio management standards.

Next, the PPMS Team looked at whether the two subjects should be combined as one standard or treated separately. A sub-team was formed to perform a literature survey and poll the PM community to determine the differences and similarities between program and portfolio management processes. The research confirmed that while program management processes provide for the management of a group of interdependent projects, portfolio management comprises continuous, repeatable, and sustainable processes designed to map business requirements and objectives to projects and programs. As a result of this investigation, the PPMS Team concluded that the profession would be best served with two standards.

Despite the differences in these processes, the PPMS Team believed that because of the relationships between the two subjects and that these were first time standards, it would be best to manage them both under one program. The PPMS Core Team proposed this approach to the SPT, which approved the recommendation. In kind, the PPMS Team developed detailed requirements for each standard that the SPT also approved. The Core Team developed a program plan and general team orientation, which was mandatory, to help volunteers engage effectively. Development of both standards began in early 2004.

B.3 Drafting *The Standard for Program Management*

The Program Management Architecture Team (ProgMAT), jointly led by Clarese Walker and David Whelbourn, organized into four sub-teams: one for each chapter (1-3) and integration.

The team recognized early that the processes for program management closely paralleled those of project management, but were larger in scope. In addition, program management further distinguished itself by containing three broad themes that are common throughout each program: benefits management, stakeholder management and governance.

While most of the work was done virtually, the team gathered for a meeting in Philadelphia in October 2004 to finalize the document. In the last quarter of 2004, the ProgMAT's draft standard underwent separate reviews by the PPMS Edit and Quality Teams in preparation for a broader review by, potentially, the whole PPMS Team. This broader review emulated the eventual global exposure draft review that PMI would conduct. The "mini-exposure draft" process generated over 400 comments from PPMS volunteers around the world.

The ProgMAT's work benefited from these comments and recommendations in the improvement or confirmation of content, even though a significant number of comments received were editorial. In general, this internal exposure draft process validated that the ProgMAT's draft was on target, as reviewers did not identify any major gaps.

B.4 Delivering the First *Standard for Program Management*

The PPMS Core Team guided the final revisions and submitted the revised version to the general PPMS Team for a consensus vote. The overwhelming majority of those voting indicated acceptance of the proposed standard without reservation. The Core

Team approved the proposed standard before turning it over to the SPT for review and approval in March 2005. The SPT engaged independent subject matter experts to augment the review process. From there, minor refinements were made and the proposed standard went on to a 90-day exposure draft process starting in June 2005.

The exposure draft period for *The Standard for Program Management* ended August 19, 2005. PMI received 465 comments that the PPMS Adjudication Team reviewed. More than half of these comments were accepted, accepted with modification, or identified for review in the next version of the standard. The PPMS Core Team approved the actions of the Adjudication Team and directed the final edit and approval of the proposed standard. Only one adjudication action was appealed, and PMI's Adjudication Appeals Team subsequently resolved it.

In December 2005, the PPMS Core Team transferred the final draft for approval by the PMI Standards Consensus Body and subsequent publication.

Appendix C

Contributors and Reviewers of *The Standard for Program Management*

This appendix lists, alphabetically within groupings, those individuals who have contributed to the development and production of *The Standard for Program Management*. No simple list or even multiple lists can adequately portray all the contributions of those who have volunteered to develop *The Standard for Program Management*. Appendix B describes specific contributions of many of the individuals listed below and should be consulted for further information about individual contributions to the project.

The Project Management Institute is grateful to all of these individuals for their support and acknowledges their contributions to the project management profession.

C.1 *The Standard for Program Management* Project Core Team

The following individuals served as members, were contributors of text or concepts, and served as leaders within the Project Core Team (PCT):

David W. Ross, PMP, Project Manager
Paul E. Shaltry, PMP, Deputy Project
  Manager
Claude Emond, MBA, PMP
Larry Goldsmith, MBA, PMP
Nancy Hildebrand, BSc, PMP
Jerry Manas, PMP

Patricia G. Mulcair, PMP
Beth Ouellette, PMP
Tom E. Vanderheiden, PMP
Clarese Walker, PMP
David Whelbourn, MBA, PMP
Michael A. Yinger

C.2 Significant Contributors

In addition to the members of the Project Core Team, the following individuals provided significant input or concepts:

Fred Abrams, PMP, CPL
Greg Alexander, PhD, PE
Ronald L. Anderson, PMP, MPM
A. Kent Bettisworth
Peggy J. Brady, PMP
Nancy A. Cygan, PMP
Jeffrey J. Dworkin, PMP
Harold S. Hunt, PMP
Mary M. Kosovich, PMP, PE
Polisetty Veera Subrahmanya Kumar, PMP
Cheryl D. Logan, PMP

J. Kendall Lott, PMP
Angela Lummel, PMP
Susan MacAndrew, MBA, PMP
Russell McDowell, M. Eng., PMP
Laura L. Miller, PMP
Crispin (Kik) Piney, PMP
Clare J. Settle, PMP
Srikanth U.S MS, PMP
Nageswaran Vaidyanathan, PMP
Thomas Walenta, PMP

C.3 *The Standard for Program Management* Project Team Members

In addition to those listed above, the following Program Management Team Members provided input to and recommendations on drafts of *The Standard for Program Management*:

Mohamed Hosney Abdelgelil
Pankaj Agrawal, PMP, CISA
Eduardo O. Aguilo, PMP
Zubair Ahmed, PMP
Mounir A. Ajam, MS, PMP
Joyce Alexander
Petya Alexandrova, PMP
Shelley M. Alton, MBA, PMP
Luis E. Alvarez Dionisi, MS, PMP
Neelu Amber
Cynthia Anderson, PMP
Mauricio Andrade, PMP
Jayant Aphale, Ph.D., MBA
Michael Appleton, CMC, PMP
V. Alberto Araujo, MBA, PMP
Jose Carlos Arce Rioboo, PMP
Alexey O. Arefiev, PMP
Mario Arlt, PMP
Julie Arnold, PMP
Canan Z. Aydemir
Darwyn S. Azzinaro, PMP
AC Fred Baker, PMP, MBA
Rod Baker, MAPM, CPM
Lorie A. Ballbach, PMP
Harold Wayne Balsinger
Keith E. Bandt, PMP
Kate Bankston, PMP
Anil Bansal

Christina Barbosa, PMP
John P. Benfield, PMP
Randy Bennett, PMP, RCC
David D. Bigness, Jr.
Susan S. Bivins, PMP
Jeroen Bolluijt
Dave M. Bond, Ph.D., PMP
Stephen F. Bonk, PMP, P.E.
Herbert Borchardt, PMP
Ann Abigail Bosacker, PMP
Christine M. Boudreau
Laurent Bour, PMP
Lynda Bourne, DPM, PMP
Mark E. Bouska, PMP
Sonia Boutari, PMP
David Bradford, PMP
Adrienne L. Bransky, PMP
Donna Brighton, PMP
Shirley F. Buchanan, PMP
Matthew Burrows, MIMC, PMP
Jacques Cantin
James D. Carlin, PMP
Margareth F. Santos Carneiro, PMP, MsC.
Brian R. Carter, PMP
Jose M. Carvalho, PMP
Pietro Casanova, PMP
Trevor Chappell, FIEE, PMP
Gordon Chastain

Deepak Chauhan, PMP, APM
Eshan S. Chawla, MBA, PMP
Keith Chiavetta
Jaikumar R. Chinnakonda, PMP
Edmond Choi
Sandra Ciccolallo
Lisa Clark
Kurt J. Clemente Sr., PMP
Jose Correia Alberto, M.Sc., LCGI
April M. Cox, PMP
Mark R. Cox, PMP
Margery J. Cruise, M.Sc., PMP
Damyan Georgiev Damyanov
Kiran M. Dasgupta, MBA, PMP
Sushovan Datta
Kenneth M. Daugherty, PMP
Stephanie E. Dawson, PMP
Pallab K. Deb, B Tech, MBA
Nikunj Desai
D. James Dickson, PMP
Christopher DiFilippo, PMP
Peter Dimov, PMP, CBM
Vivek Dixit
Janet Dixon, PMP, Ed.D.
Ross Domnik, PMP
Anna Dopico, PMP
Jim C. Dotson, PMP
Karthik Duddala
Renee De Mond
Karen K. Dunlap, PMP, SSGB
Charles A. Dutton, PMP
Lowell D. Dye, PMP
Barbara S. Ebner
Daniella Eilers
Michael G. Elliott
Michael T. Enea, PMP, CISSP
Michael P. Ervick, MBA, PMP
Clifton D. Fauntroy
Linda A. Fernandez, MBA
Ezequiel Ferraz, PMP
Maviese A. Fisher, PMP, IMBA
Joyce M. Flavin, PMP
Jacqueline Flores, PMP
Robert J. Forster, MCPM, PMP
Carolyn A. Francis, PMP
Serena E. Frank, PMP
Kenneth Fung, PMP, MBA
Lorie Gibbons, PMP
Lisa Ann Giles, PMP
John Glander
Sunil Kumar Goel, PMP

Victor Edward Gomes, BSc, PMP
Andres H. Gonzalez D., ChE
Mike Goodman, PMP, MSEE
Ferdousi J. Gramling
Alicia Maria Granados
Bjoern Greiff, PMP
Steve Gress, PMP
Naveen Grover
Yvonne D. Grymes
Claude L. Guertin, BSc, PMP
Papiya Gupta
Bulent E. Guzel, PMP
Deng Hao
Cheryl Harris-Barney
Holly Hickman
David A. Hillson, PhD, PMP
MD Hudon, PMP
Sandy Yiu Fai Hui
Zeeshan Idrees, BSc.
Isao Indo, PMP, PE.JP
Andrea Innocenti, PMP
Suhail Iqbal, PE, PMP
Anshoom Jain, PMP
Venkata Rao Jammi, MBA, PMP
David B. Janda
Haydar Jawad, PMP
G. Lynne Jeffries, PMP
Monique Jn-Marie, PMP
Kenneth L. Jones, Jr., PMP
Martin H. Kaerner, Dr.-Ing.
Craig L. Kalsa, PMP
Kenday Samuel Kamara
Michael Kamel, PEng, PMP
Malle Kancherla, PMP
Soundaian Kamalakannan
Saravanan Nanjan Kannan, PMP
Barbara Karten, PMP
Ashish Kemkar, PMP
Geoffrey L. Kent, PMP
Todd M. Kent, PMP
Thomas C. Keuten, PMP, CMC
Sandeep Khanna, MBA, PMP
Karu Godwin Kirijath
Raymond R. Klosek, PMP
Richard M. Knaster, PMP
Victoria Kosuda
Koushik Sudeendra, PMP
Narayan Krish, PMP, MS
S V R Madhu Kumar, MBA, PMP
Puneet Kumar
Girish Kurwalkar, PMP

Janet Kuster, PMP, MBA

Puneet Kuthiala, PMP

Olaronke Arike Ladipo, MD

Guilherme Ponce de Leon S. Lago, PMP

Robert LaRoche, PMP

David W. Larsen, PMP

Terry Laughlin, PMP

Fernando Ledesma, PM, MBA

Ade Lewandowski

Corazon B. Lewis, PMP

Jeffrey M. Lewman, PMP

Lynne C. Limpert, PMP

Giri V. Lingamarla, PMP

Dinah Lucre

Douglas Mackey, PMP

Saji Madapat, PMP, CSSMBB

Erica Dawn Main

Subbaraya N. Mandya, PMP

Ammar W. Mango, PMP, CSSBB

Tony MaramaraHal Markowitz

Franck L. Marle, PhD, PMP

Sandeep Mathur, PMP, MPD

Dean R. MayerWarren V. Mayo, PMP, CSSBB

Philippe Mayrand, PMP

Yves Mboda, PMP

Amy McCarthy

Richard C. McClarty, Sr.

Eric McCleaf, PMP

Malcolm McFarlane

Graham McHardy

Christopher F. McLoon

Kevin Patrick McNalley, PMP

David McPeters, PMP

Carl J. McPhail, PMP

Vladimir I. Melnik, M.sC., PMP

Philip R. Mileham

M. Aslam Mirza, MBA, PMP

Rahul Mishra

Nahid Mohammadi MS

Sandhya Mohanraj, PMP

Subrata Mondal

Donald James Moore

Balu Moothedath

Roy E. Morgan, P.E., PMP

Sharon D. Morgan-Redmond, PMP

Saradhi Motamarri, MTech, PMP

Dr. Ralf Muller, PMP

Seetharam Mukkavilli, Ph.D., PMP

Praveen Chand Mullacherry, PMP

Kannan Sami Nadar, PMP

Sreenikumar G. Nair

Vinod B. Nair, B Tech, MBA

Carlos Roberto Naranjo P, PMP

Nigel Oliveira, PMP, BBA

Sean O'Neill, PMP

Bradford Orcutt, PMP

Rolf A. Oswald, PMP

Louis R. Pack, PMP

Sukanta Kumar Padhi, PMP

Lennox A. Parkins, MBA, PMP

Anil Peer, P.Eng., PMP

Sameer K. Penakalapati, PMP

Zafeiris K. Petalas Ph.D. Candidate

Susan Philipose

D. Michele Pitman

Charles M. Poplos, Ed.D., PMP

Todd Porter

Ranganath Prabhu, PMP

Yves Pszenica, PMP

Sridhar Pydah, PMP

Peter Quinnell, MBA

Sueli S. Rabaca, PMP

Madhubala Rajagopal, MCA, PMP

Mahalingam Ramamoorthi, PMP

Sameer S. Ramchandani, PMP

Jay R. Ramsuchit, PMP

Prem G. Ranganath, PMP, CSQE

Raju N. Rao, PMP, SCPM

Tony Raymond, PMP

Carolyn S. Reid, PMP, MBA

Geoff Reiss, FAPM, M.Phil

Bill Rini, PMP

Steven F. Ritter, PMP

Cynthia Roberts

Andrew C. Robison, PMP

Allan S. Rodger, PMP

Randy T. Rohovit

Dennis M. Rose, PMP

Jackson Rovina, PMP

Julie Rundgren

Diana Russo, PMP

Gunes Sahillioglu, MSc, MAPM

Banmeet Kaur Saluja, PMP

Mansi A. Sanap

Nandakumar Sankaran

Kulasekaran C. Satagopan, PMP, CQM

Gary Scherling, PMP, ITIL

John Schmitt, PMP

Neils (Chris) Schmitt

Mark N. Scott

Stephen F. Seay, PMP

Sunita Sekhar, PMP

David Seto, PMP
Nandan Shah, PMP
Shoukat M. Sheikh
Donna- Mae Shyduik
Derry Simmel, PMP, MBA
Arun Singh, PMP, CSQA
Deepak Singh, PMP
Anand Sinha
Ron Sklaver, PMP, CISA
Michael I. Slansky, PMP
Nancy A. Slater, MBA, PMP
Christopher Sloan
Dennis M. SmithNoel Smyth
Jamie B. Solak, M.A.Ed.
Keith J. Spacek
Gomathy Srinivasan, PMP
Srinivasan Govindarajulu, PMP
Joyce Statz, Ph.D., PMP
Marie Sterling, PMP
Martin B. Stivers, PMP
Curtis A. Stock, PMP
Michael E. Stockwell
LeConte F. Stover, MBA, PMP
Anthony P. Strande
Juergen Sturany, PMP
Kalayani Subramanyan, PMP
Mohammed Suheel, BE, MCP
Patricia Sullivan-Taylor, MPA, PMP
Vijay Suryanarayana, PMP
Dawn C. Sutherland, PMP
Alexander M. Tait
Martin D. Talbott, PMP

Ali Taleb, MBA, PMP
David E. Taylor, PMP
Sai K. Thallam, PMP
Ignatius Thomas, PMP
James M. Toney, Jr.
Eugenio R. Tonin, PMP
Jonathan Topp
Murthy TS, PMP
Shi-Ja Sophie Tseng, PMP
Yen K. TuIan Turnbull
Dr. M. Ulagaraj, Ph.D.
Marianne Utendorf, PMP
Ernest C. Valle, M.B.A., PMP
Thierry Vanden Broeck, PMP
Gary van Eck, PMP
Paula Ximena Varas, PMP
Jayadeep A. Vijayan, B Tech, MBA
Alberto Villa, PMP, MBA
Ludmila Volkovich
Namita Wadhwa, CAPM
Jane B. Walton, CPA
Yongjiang Wang, PMP
Michael Jeffrey Watson
Kevin R. Wegryn, PMP, MA
Richard A. Weller, PMP
Thomas Williamson, PMP
Rick Woods, MBA, PMP
Fan Wu
Cai Ding Zheng, PMP
Yuchen Zhu, PMP
Leon Zilber, MSc, PMP

C.4 Final Exposure Draft Reviewers and Contributors

In addition to team members, the following individuals provided recommendations for improving *The Standard for Program Management*:

Hussain Ali Al-Ansari, Eur Ing, C Eng.
Mohammed Abdulla Al-Kuwari, PMP, C Eng.
Mohammed Safi Batley, MIM
Colin S. Cantlie, PMP, P.Eng.
John M. Clifford, CAPM
John E. Cormier, PMP
Gary C. Davis, PMP
Johan Delaure, PMP
Jean-Luc Frere, Ir, PMP
Stanislaw Gasik
Harsh Grover, PMP
Charles L. Hunt
Matthew D. Kraft, PMP
Craig J. Letavec, PMP
Susan Marshall
Yan Bello Mendez, PMP
Sundara Nagarajan
Kazuhiko Okubo, PMP, PE

Jerry Partridge, PMP
Kenyon D. Potter, PE, JD
Kenneth P. Schlatter
Gregory P. Schneider, PMP
Kazuo Shimizu, PMP
Larry Sieck
Jennie R. Smith, PMP
Martin B. Stivers, PMP
George Sukumar
Craig M. Thiel, PMP
Srikanth U.S MS, PMP
Judy L. Van Meter
Dave Violette, MPM, PMP
William P. Wampler, PMP
CD Watson, PMP
Patrick Weaver, PMP, FAICD
Rebecca A. Winston, Esq.

C.5 PMI Project Management Standards Program Member Advisory Group

The following individuals served as members of the PMI Standards Program Member Advisory Group during development of *The Standard for Program Management*:

Julia M. Bednar, PMP
Carol Holliday, PMP
Thomas Kurihara
Debbie O'Bray

Asbjorn Rolstadas, Ph.D.
Cyndi Stackpole
Bobbye Underwood, PMP
Dave Violette, MPM, PMP

C.6 Production Staff

Special mention is due to the following employees of PMI:

Ruth Anne Guerrero, PMP, Standards Manager
Dottie Nichols, PMP, Former Standards Manager
Kristin L. Vitello, Standards Project Specialist
Nan Wolfslayer, Standards Project Specialist
Dan Goldfischer, Editor-in-Chief
Richard E. Schwartz, Product Editor
Barbara Walsh, Publications Planner

Appendix D

Program Management Tools and Techniques

Common tools and techniques can be thought of as common practice. They are those influences on the processes that the program team brings to the program. Among the tools and techniques common for many program management processes are those presented below.

1. **Expert Judgment**

   Expert judgment may be obtained from a variety of sources both internal and external to the program. These sources often include functional and technical area specialists assigned to the program and in other organizational units within the enterprise, external consultants, professional and technical associations, and specialized governmental and industry bodies.

2. **Meetings**

   All Program Management Process Groups require some form of deliberation and discussion before decisions are made or output of a process is achieved. Meetings can be face-to-face or in a virtual setting. Since many of the program management processes require participation from various personnel, groups or functions, conducting meetings serves as an effective technique that provides benefits from the synergistic approach taken.

3. **Reviews**

   Reviews are typically internal activities such as management or peer reviews conducted before communicating with program stakeholders. Reviews can take other forms as well.

   Project reviews provide insight into status and plans for each project and the impact on the overall program. As stated in Chapter 1, benefit reviews are also very important to ensure that the outlined benefit process is followed, and that each benefit is being monitored and tracked effectively.

   Phase gate reviews are carried out at key decision points in the program life cycle to provide an independent assessment of the status of the program and to provide an assurance that identified critical success factors, best practices, and program risks are being addressed.

4. Policies and Procedures

Policies and procedures serve to implement standards, processes, and work methods, resulting in the completion of the work required by the program. Policies and procedures cover classification of information, restrictions on distribution, and requirements for retention. Organizational policies dictate required contents of a program management artifact such as a plan, the specific methodology used to create the artifact, and the approval process for the artifact.

Risk responses may include taking steps to mitigate or avoid a risk, developing plans to be carried out if a risk becomes real, transferring a risk by means such as subcontracting or third-party insurance or accepting the risk. Conversely, risk responses may include an effort to increase the likelihood of capitalizing on known opportunities.

It is important that the program management involvement in risk should support the risk activities of the program component. Program-specific risk activities include the following:

- Identifying inter-project risks;
- Reviewing the risk response plans of the component projects for proposed actions that could affect other component projects—and modifying them as needed;
- Determining root causes at a multi-project level;
- Proposing solutions to risks escalated by component project managers;
- Implementing response mechanisms that benefit more than one component project;
- Managing a contingency reserve (in terms of cost and/or time) consolidated across the entire program.

Appendix E

Benefits Assurance and Sustainment

E.1 Purpose

This appendix addresses aspects of program management beyond the multi-project management and benefits management that are the main focus of this standard. These other aspects are firmly grounded in previous project management standards but apply less universally in program management organizations.

E.2 Background

The 1996 and 2000 editions of the *PMBOK® Guide* addressed programs in paragraph 1.5 defining a program as "a group of projects managed in a coordinated way to obtain benefits not available from managing them individually. Many programs also include elements of ongoing operations." These editions of the Guide listed examples which included "ongoing manufacturing and support . . . in the field" along with the project elements which design and deliver the product. These editions went on to cite other examples that include multiple releases over time and repetitive or cyclical undertakings.

The *PMBOK® Guide*—Third Edition and the *Organizational Project Management Maturity Model* (*OPM3®*) standard use the same definition of Program, which is changed from the earlier editions of the *PMBOK® Guide*. The first sentence remains unchanged while the second sentence was revised to say, "Programs may include elements of related work outside the scope of the discrete projects in the program." This broader definition is consistent with and does not exclude the "ongoing operations" aspects cited in the earlier *PMBOK® Guide* editions.

While the examples given in the third edition no longer include "support in the field," they continue to refer to multiple releases and the repetitive or cyclical undertakings. The intent is confirmed in *OPM3* paragraph 4.4 which states that "The linking of Program Management to ongoing operations positions it as more inclusive than Project Management, and indicates a greater involvement with the general management of the organization and other management disciplines." *OPM3* goes on to say that, in addition to multi-project management, program management is also differentiated from project management by "elements of ongoing operations, such as post deployment management of the products and services produced and deployed by the program" and notes that "Program Management may include the entire product life cycle considerations such as upgrades or additional releases."

The *OPM3* standard goes on to note that "Ongoing operations may include several recurring or administrative functions that are the responsibility of the program, such as supplier relationship and equipment maintenance" and can include "the ongoing activity of monitoring and ensuring the benefits expected of the program." *OPM3* offers specific guidance to its use in the area of program management stating that use of its best practices and capabilities must consider both aspects—multi-project management and product-related.

E.3 Assuring and Sustaining Benefits

In the context of Program Management, as used in the main body of *The Standard for Program Management*, programs focus on benefits. The ongoing activities discussed above can be said to focus on *benefits assurance* during the continuing delivery and *benefits sustainment* during the field support of the product. Each project, by *PMBOK® Guide* definition, is responsible for the creation and delivery of a product, service or result the completion of which defines the end point in the project life cycle. Programs, on the other hand, can continue beyond the project life cycle to continue the delivery or deployment of the product developed by a project. This program activity focuses on management activities such as production of additional product and the preparation of additional customers to receive and use the product.

Clearly, the groundwork for ongoing deployment must be laid by the *project* during its life cycle, but the activity involved in continued deployment and sustaining the benefits after deployment is beyond the scope of the project. It is an inherent element of *project* management to ensure that the intended customer can use and maintain the product. This levies a responsibility for product support planning and execution on most projects.

The responsibility for benefits sustainment (product support) to ensure that the customer remains able to use and maintain and that the product continues to deliver the benefits expected by the customer falls outside the traditional project life cycle, but very often within the program life cycle. While it may follow a structured approach, ongoing product support does not usually define its work with a WBS and control activities such as earned value management are generally not applicable. Program Management of ongoing product support can entail the following activities:

- Monitoring the performance of the product from a reliability and availability-for-use perspective and comparing that performance to that predicted during the development of the product.
- Monitoring the continued suitability of the deployed product to provide the benefits expected by the customers owning and operating it. This can include the continued viability of interface with other products and the continued completeness of the product functionality.
- Monitoring the continued availability of logistics support for the product in light of technology advancements and the willingness of vendors to continue to support older configurations.
- Directly responding to customer inputs on their needs for product support assistance or for improvements in performance or functionality
- Providing on-demand support for the product either in parts, improved technical information or real-time help desk support.

- Planning for and establishing operational support of the product separate from the program management function without relinquishing the other product support functions.
- Initiating new projects to respond to operational issues with the deployed product being supported. Such issues can include the need to improve reliability problems, address software anomalies, update configurations to ensure continued effective interface with other products or to provide additional functionality to meet evolving requirements.
- Initiating new projects to respond to logistics issues with the deployed product being supported. Such issues can include the continued ability to support a physical product or associated support equipment with spare parts which may require engineering retrofit changes to ensure continued supportability.
- Updating technical information concerning the product in response to frequent product support queries.
- Planning the transition of product support from program management to an operations function within the organization.
- Planning the retirement and disposition of the product or the cessation of product support with appropriate guidance to the current customers.

E.4 Organizational Differences

Some organizations consider these aspects of program management to be the responsibility of operational management functions and the nature of this distinction between operational and program management hence differs from organization to organization. In some product-oriented organizations, a program team is continually monitoring the performance of, and customer satisfaction with delivered products.

Such organizations use program management to coordinate the processes of performance assurance, launching of new projects to improve products or satisfy emerging customer desires, and ongoing delivery of products both baseline and improved. Other organizations separate the functions of product development, production/delivery, and product support depending on an operations element to maintain contact with customers using the product and expecting them to identify the need for project activity to improve products or create new products in response to emerging demand.

Still others maintain a close working relationship between program and operational management, but ensure that the functions and responsibilities are separate after some point in time in the product life cycle. In most cases, the functions of product support from a logistics perspective are separated from program management once the project or program has ensured the successful deployment of a properly supported product.

E.5 Critical Success Factors

Critical success factors associated with these ongoing benefits assurance and sustainment elements include:
- Assuring that, in the project and program environments, the creation of a new product or service is accompanied by the development and deployment of support for that output.

- Assuring that the demands for continuing delivery/deployment are understood so that resources can be appropriately applied to maintain the schedule and satisfy customer expectations.
- Assuring that ongoing product support adds value by managing the post-production product life cycle. The value added by that management must be greater than the cost of management. Since every product has a life cycle and every project has a beginning and end (is a temporary endeavor), project management principles can be leveraged to increase value within the program.
- Assuring that upstream projects (the performing organization or the project that creates the product) define and otherwise provide life-cycle information to support benefits sustainment (product support) for management of the product life cycle.
- Assuring that there is ongoing benchmarking of support practices.
- Assuring that ongoing product support representation is present at beginning of the project that produces the product.
- Assuring that there is a customer support organization.
- Assuring that support is properly scheduled when changes are made to the deployed product so that customers will be able to support the updated products.
- Assuring the availability of training for support staff to understand product support requirements.
- Assuring that repair/return facilities/processes requirements are developed and implemented.

Program managers performing product support need to be conversant in a wide range of quality and logistics disciplines:
- Reliability and Maintainability (R&M)—Program managers need to understand the differences between measuring R&M during the developmental phases when such measures usually result from laboratory testing under controlled conditions and the operational environment where the customer is concerned with availability of the product for use and can consider all unexpected maintenance actions as failures. The program manager also needs to understand the processes for determining the effectiveness of a scheduled maintenance program and optimizing such a program.
- Integrated Logistics Support (ILS)—Program managers need to understand the elements of integrated logistics support so that they can be properly managed for products in operational use by customers. These elements include spares support, support equipment, technical data, packaging/handling/storage/transportation, training, training equipment and facilities. Program managers also need to understand how to respond to customer experience with the products to properly influence redesign efforts to correct problems.
- Configuration Management (CM)—Program managers dealing with deployed products need to ensure that configuration management efforts consider maintaining the supportability of the products when changes are being fielded either forward in production or via retrofit of already fielded products. It is essential to consider that updated support must be made available on a schedule pacing the actual deployment of the changed end items. The requirement for new configuration equipment and support for training of personnel prior to fielding for operational use must be considered. The program manager must be able to effectively plan and manage retrofit efforts.

Appendix F

Program Management Controls

The Project Management Institute's *Organizational Project Management Maturity Model* (*OPM3®*) Knowledge Foundation introduced a new attribute for program management processes called "controls." *OPM3* defines controls as, *activities, policies or procedures that govern the execution of the process, so that the process operates in a consistent, predictable manner*. Program management controls can be thought of as common knowledge. They are those influences on the processes that the program team brings to the program.

Chapter 3 of *The Standard for Program Management* does not associate specific controls with the program management processes described therein. However, because of the importance of this concept, this appendix provides a general discussion of the role played by controls with respect to the program management processes. Among the controls applicable to many program management processes are those below.

A. **Standards**

Industry and trade associations, governmental bodies, including the military, and other groups have developed widely recognized and accepted standards, often international in scope. Where applicable, these standards may be invoked in contractual documents prepared by a procuring agency for a program. Standards may also be developed specifically for a program and may include quality standards, schedule standards, training standards, and work breakdown structure standards.

B. **Policies and Procedures**

Policies and procedures implement standards, processes, and work methods that result in the work required by the program being performed. They cover classification of information, restrictions on distribution, and requirements for retention. Organizational policies dictate required contents of a program management artifact such as a plan, the specific methodology used to create the artifact, and approval process for the artifact.

C. **Program Plans**

Typically, a program is driven by a strategic plan, which includes the statement of the business goals for the program. All work in a program should contribute to one or more business goals. Business goals are the criteria against which potential program activities are judged.

Various plans are generally encompassed in a program management plan, which formulates and documents the management strategy and approach for the program. The program management plan comprises a number of subsidiary management plans, such as a:

- Cost management plan
- Communications management plan
- Procurement management plan
- Quality management plan
- Resource management plan
- Risk management plan
- Schedule management plan
- Scope management plan
- Staffing management plan.

These and other subsidiary management plans may be incorporated directly into the same document as the program management plan or may exist as individual document artifacts.

D. Reviews

Reviews are typically internal activities such as management or peer reviews with their outcomes communicated to program stakeholders.

Reviews are executed as controls on numerous program management processes in all of the Program Process Groups. Reviews may include periodic program risk reviews and program management reviews, including phase-gate reviews as noted in Chapter 2. Reviews of projects within the program provide insight into status and plans for each project and the impact on the overall program.

E. Oversight

Oversight by an executive review board or an individual executive may cause modifications to the program if the overarching business or strategic needs change. Executive oversight plays the key role in evaluating the proposed program management plan with respect to the business objectives and constraints. Resource contention at the program level will typically involve other programs or activities outside of the program. These are the responsibility of first the stakeholders and then the executive level of the organization. Oversight is required during estimating and budgeting to ensure that they are well within limits of overall organizational plans. Oversight bodies often include change control boards with the authority to approve changes to the program's scope, budget, and schedule.

Oversight controls should result in sign-off by the stakeholder to confirm that the requirements to be met by the program are both necessary and sufficient to successfully perform the stakeholder's function.

F. Audits

Audits may be an internal control or may be an activity imposed by the client. In either case, the audit would require that information distributed be substantiated by stored program information from which reports and distributions were compiled. Additionally, audits could require demonstration of a process that meets certain criteria as spelled out in the contract or agreement. Types of audits may include: control point audits, financial audits, process audits, risk response audits, and quality audits.

G. Contracts

Standard contractual terms and conditional clauses may be pre-developed and approved for inclusion in contracts awarded by a procuring agency. These may be specific to an enterprise or in the case of government agencies may apply to all government contracts awarded.

H. Directories and Distribution Lists

Standard lists are established and maintained to control the routing and recipients of all of the formal communications and messages sent to program stakeholders. This may include documents, presentations, reports, and memoranda in electronic or paper media, electronic mail, information uploaded to web sites, and information to be formally transmitted by other means and media.

I. Documentation

Documentation controls may include requiring that all formal documents relating to the program conform to style guides and documentation templates to be created and used for documentation of a repetitive nature, such as plans, specifications and periodic reports.

J. Regulations

Regulations may stipulate the collection of pertinent data. Regulations can include environmental legislation, government regulations and laws, legal opinions, legislative requirements, legislative restrictions, organizational legislation, and regulations regarding the sale or disposal of equipment, facilities, or other property.

Appendix G

Examples of Organizational Structuring of Programs

Section 1.6 addresses program management in relation to organizational planning. The relationships between portfolios, programs and projects, as illustrated in Figure 1-2 of Section 1.4, not only establishes the differences between the three entities, but the organizational implications as well. Depending on the organization's acceptance of portfolio management, similar business situations could conceivably result in the establishment of one or several programs.

Take, for example, an organization that has project portfolios and whose strategic business plan identifies three strategic initiatives:
- Develop a new customer base
- Focus on growth revenue options
- Develop a new product line.

The initiative to develop a new product line is the highest priority and two programs are initiated to deliver the expected outlined benefits. The relationship between the portfolio, programs and projects is depicted in Figure G-1.

On the other hand, if the organization is not using portfolio management, the relationship might consider the program as the highest level of the hierarchy. Therefore, the relationship between the business plan, programs and projects is as displayed in Figure G-2, where the new product line initiative triggers a single program.

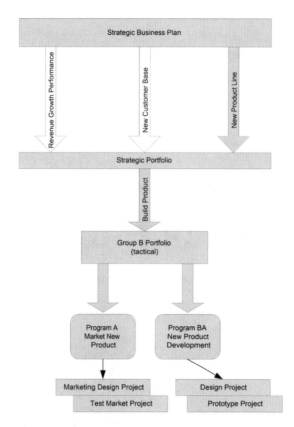

Figure G-1. Relationships among Portfolios and Programs

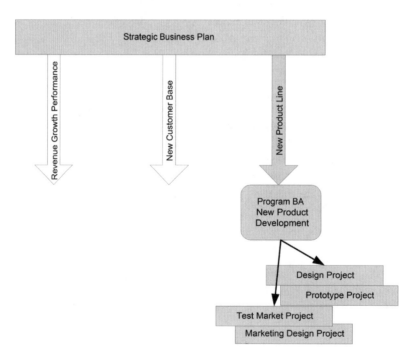

Figure G-2. Program Strategic Initiative Context

Appendix H

Variance From or Extensions to Other Related PMI Standards

The Standard for Program Management has been preceded by two authoritative standards published by the Project Management Institute (PMI). These are *A Guide to the Project Management Body of Knowledge (PMBOK® Guide)*—Third Edition and the *Organizational Project Management Maturity Model (OPM3®)*.

The *PMBOK® Guide*—Third Edition addresses only project management processes, the Project Domain, but served as a reference point for developing *The Standard for Program Management*. The variances between the two standards are discussed below in Section H.1.

OPM3 introduced the concept of program management processes, the Program Domain, and described them briefly in Appendix I of that document, with the expectation that this standard would expand and elaborate upon them. The variances between this standard and *OPM3* are discussed in Section H.2.

H.1 Comparison of *The Standard for Program Management* and *PMBOK® Guide*—Third Edition Processes

A Guide to the Project Management Body of Knowledge (PMBOK® Guide)—Third Edition addresses project management and is the generally accepted standard for project management processes. As a companion standard, *The Standard for Program Management* addresses program management and focuses on the processes that apply to program management. Although these processes are similar to project management processes in many respects, they are not equivalent to them.

Whereas the *PMBOK® Guide*—Third Edition identifies 44 project management processes, this standard identifies 39 processes for program management. Furthermore, not all of these processes are the same. Table H-1 provides a comparison of the two sets of processes.

Program management and project management processes may have many similarities at the descriptive level. However, there are very significant differences in program management process inputs, controls, outputs and tools and techniques and the inputs, outputs and tools and techniques associated with project management processes. These differences are too extensive to detail here but a comparison of the two

	Program Management Processes	Project Management Processes
Initiating Process Group	• Initiate Program • Authorize Projects • Initiate Team	• Develop Project Charter • Develop Preliminary Scope Statement
Planning Process Group	• Develop Program Management Plan • Scope Definition • Create Program WBS • Schedule Development • Cost Estimating and Budgeting • Quality Planning • Human Resource Planning • Communications Planning • Plan Program Purchases and Acquisitions • Plan Program Contracting • Risk Management Planning and Analysis • Interface Planning • Transition Planning • Resource Planning	• Develop Project Management Plan • Scope Planning • Scope Definition • Create WBS • Activity Definition • Activity Sequencing • Activity Resource Estimating • Activity Duration Estimating • Schedule Development • Cost Estimating • Cost Budgeting • Quality Planning • Human Resource Planning • Communications Planning • Risk Management Planning • Risk Identification • Qualitative Risk Analysis • Quantitative Risk Analysis • Risk Response Planning • Plan Purchase and Acquisitions • Plan Contracting
Executing Process Group	• Direct and Manage Program Execution • Perform Quality Assurance • Acquire Program Team • Develop Program Team • Information Distribution • Request Seller Responses • Select Sellers	• Direct and Manage Project Execution • Perform Quality Assurance • Acquire Project Team • Develop Project Team • Information Distribution • Request Seller Responses • Select Sellers
Monitoring and Controlling Process Group	• Monitor and Control Program Work • Integrated Change Control • Scope Control • Schedule Control • Cost Control • Perform Quality Control • Performance Reporting • Risk Monitoring and Control • Program Contract Administration • Resource Control • Issue Management and Control • Communications Control	• Monitor and Control Project Work • Integrated Change Control • Scope Verification • Scope Control • Schedule Control • Cost Control • Perform Quality Control • Manage Project Team • Performance Reporting • Manage Stakeholders • Risk Monitoring and Control • Contract Administration
Closing Process Group	• Close Program • Contract Closure • Component Closure	• Close Project • Contract Closure

Table H-1. Comparison of *The Standard for Program Management* and *PMBOK® Guide*—Third Edition Processes

standards will quickly reveal many of them. This is attributable to the differences in the roles played by processes for program management and those of project management processes. Program management processes operate on a broader scale and at a higher level than project management processes and must accommodate the management of multiple projects within a program at any given point of time. This is further complicated in that different projects in the program may be in different life cycle phases concurrently and program management processes must allow for this situation.

H.2 Program Differences

While there are many similarities between programs and projects in the activities required for planning at this stage of the life cycle, there are some key differences between programs and projects.

Programs are made up of a variety of projects. In the same manner that the program needed to go through a selection/approval stage, generally the projects that make up the program will likewise need to be approved and prioritized. This project selection may also have to take into account any interdependencies of the projects. This implies that the program will either define a project selection criterion or will use one that the organization already has in place. Either way, the program will need to consider the projects that it will formulate and initiate for the solution, and track any work required to get them through a selection process.

Program management generally must consider the full life cycle of the products/ initiatives that are being implemented. While project may be targeted at one particular aspect (e.g., development of a new financial system, or deployment of new servers/ workstations for the application), programs need to consider the entire picture.

For example, on a major computer application upgrade, the following areas should be included in the program:

- Feasibility studies for key requirements
- Development of the new version of the application system
- Project enablers such as deployment of the new hardware and software required
- Any data conversion and system transition items going from the previous version to the new application
- Life cycle support and maintenance of the application (including help desks, training, documentation, testing and configuration management systems)
- Any shutdown costs at the end of the program (will office facilities/equipment need to be sold/scrapped?)

The requirement to consider different phases during the life of the program also provides some freedom for the program manager. For example, trade-offs can be made between spending more resources during the development stage, in order to reduce costs during support (e.g., on-line tutorials); or more time in architecture may result in less hardware needing to be procured during deployment.

The duration of programs tend to be longer than that of projects. This has an impact on the planning and the management of a program in different ways compared to a project. There are greater chances of changes in:

- Staff during the program
- The sponsor's and client's organizations
- Technology during the life of the program
- The business environment (and hence requirements) during the program.

All of these potential changes mean that the management of the scope and communications processes will be of relatively greater importance and targeted at a more senior level of management during the program. With the potential changes in the organizations, the ability to maintain key senior management support is also more of a challenge.

In projects, one problem is personnel anxiety that increases towards the end of the project. With the end coming into sight, some people are concerned with what their next assignment may be. This creates a challenge to maintain the focus of the team to ensure that the project completes all of the deliverables. With the duration of programs, this can be an even greater challenge, as resources may have been on the program for a number of years or decades. As the life cycle of a program nears, these shut down issues can be even harder to deal with.

One of the capabilities of a program is that it may use feasibility studies and short-term projects to determine answers to issues and verify proposed directions. Programs will have a greater propensity to need to adjust overall direction during their life cycle than projects as they accommodate project failures, change in deliveries/schedule and negative results from feasibility studies. Likewise, programs have a better capacity to adjust to "lessons learned" during their life cycle. These all combine to require a tighter planning/adjusting approach than may be required in projects. The program may need to redo significant parts of their plan during its life cycle.

H.3 *Organizational Project Management Maturity Model*

Organizational Project Management is defined as "The application of knowledge, skills, tools and techniques to organizational activities and project, program and portfolio activities to achieve the aims of an organization through projects."[1]

In December 2003, the *Organizational Project Management Maturity Model (OPM3®)* was published by the Project Management Institute (PMI). The concept of organizational project management is based on the idea that there is a correlation between project, program and portfolio management and this has been used to develop a sequential model which will help an organization to improve its maturity and achieve its strategic objectives. Program management is one of the domains of *OPM3*.

While developing the model, and as stated by the *OPM3* Knowledge Foundation, it was recognized that knowledge of program management processes is an essential part of the route to organizational project management maturity. This aspect has been considered while stating the charter for the PPMS project. It has been mandated that the program management processes along with inputs, tools, and techniques, controls and outputs as enumerated in *OPM3* be taken as the first point of reference in developing *The Standard for Program Management*. The requirements also stated that once developed, *The Standard for Program Management* should be used to update the *OPM3* Standard during its subsequent revisions.

Therefore, developing a standard for program management will be of immense use in understanding and using a model like *OPM3* and will form an integral part of its development in future versions.

Thirty-nine program management processes were identified and defined with their inputs, tools and techniques, controls and outputs in *OPM3*. These processes, along with the project management processes contained in *A Guide to the Project Management Body of Knowledge (PMBOK® Guide)*—Third Edition served as the starting point for the further development of the program management processes contained in this standard. Table H-2 compares the program management processes in this standard with those in *OPM3*.

---

[1] *Organizational Project Management Maturity Model: Knowledge Foundation.* (2003). Newtown Square, PA: Project Management Institute, p. 173.

	Program Management Processes	OPM3-Program Domain
Initiating Process Group	• Initiate Program • Authorize Projects • Initiate Team	• Scope Initiation
Planning Process Group	• Develop Program Management Plan • Scope Definition • Create Program WBS • Schedule Development • Cost Estimating and Budgeting • Quality Planning • Human Resource Planning • Communications Planning • Plan Program Purchases and Acquisitions • Plan Program Contracting • Risk Management Planning and Analysis • Interface Planning • Transition Planning • Resource Planning	• Plan Development • Scope Planning • Scope Definition • Activity Definition • Activity Sequencing • Activity Duration Estimating • Schedule Development • Cost Estimating • Cost Budgeting • Quality Planning • Organizational Planning • Staff Acquisition • Communications Planning • Risk Management Planning • Risk Identification • Qualitative Risk Analysis • Quantitative Risk Analysis • Risk Response Planning • Procurement Planning • Solicitation Planning • Resource Planning
Executing Process Group	• Direct and Manage Program Execution • Perform Quality Assurance • Acquire Program Team • Develop Program Team • Information Distribution • Request Seller Responses • Select Sellers	• Plan Execution • Quality Assurance • Team Development • Information Distribution • Solicitation • Contract Administration • Source Selection
Monitoring and Controlling Process Group	• **Monitor and Control Program Work** • Integrated Change Control • Scope Control • Schedule Control • Cost Control • Perform Quality Control • Performance Reporting • Risk Monitoring and Control • Program Contract Administration • Resource Control • Issue Management and Control • Communications Control	 • Integrated Change Control • Scope Change Control • Scope Verification • Schedule Control • Cost Control • Quality Control • Performance Reporting • Risk Monitoring and Control
Closing Process Group	• Close Program • Contract Closure • Component Closure	• Administrative Closure • Contract Closeout

Table H-2. Comparison of *The Standard for Program Management* and *OPM3®* Program Management Processes

The program management processes defined in *OPM3* were essentially an extension of the *PMBOK® Guide*—2000 Edition project management processes. During the development of *The Standard for Program Management*, considerable further research and thought was given to the differences between program and project management. The outcome was a set of processes that do not conflict with those in *OPM3*, but are much more attuned to the nature of program management. Recognizing that programs often include multiple projects, processes have been added to initiate and conclude projects within the scope of a program. One significant difference is in the Planning Process Group where some processes have been consolidated, reflecting a higher level and less detailed planning in the Program Domain compared to the more detailed lower-level planning that takes place in the Project Domain. A second major difference is in the area of controls. In the Program Domain, control must be exercised over a far broader scope and range of activities than is the case for a single project. In addition, it was recognized that earned value management is gaining wide acceptance in the Program Management Domain and an Earned Value Control Process was added. The third significant difference is in the Closing Process Group in recognition that a program often manages a more diverse range of resources, including multiple contracts and facilities, than is usually the case with a single project.

Section IV

Glossary and Index

Glossary

Index by Keyword

Glossary

1. Inclusions and Exclusions

This glossary includes terms that are:

- Unique to program management (e.g., benefits management)
- Not unique to program management but used differently or with a narrower meaning in program management than in general everyday usage (e.g., benefit, risk).

This glossary generally does not include:

- Application or industry area-specific terms
- Terms whose uses in program management do not differ in any material way from everyday use (e. g., business outcome).

2. Common Acronyms

IPECC	The Initiating, Planning, Executing, Monitoring and Controlling, and Closing Process Groups
PMBOK®	Project Management Body of Knowledge
PMO	Program Management Office
PMO	Project Management Office

3. Definitions

Many of the words here may have broader, and in some cases different, dictionary definitions to accommodate the context of program management.

Benefit. An improvement to the running of an organization such as increased sales, reduced running costs, or reduced waste.

Benefits Management. Activities and techniques for defining, creating, maximizing, and sustaining the benefits provided by programs.

Benefits Realization Plan. A document detailing the expected benefits to be realized by a program and how these benefits will be achieved.

Business Outcome. A financial result (cost saving, opportunity, employee reduction, revenue growth, revenue retention) derived from implementing an organization's strategies.

Closing Processes [Program Management Process Group]. Those processes performed to formally terminate all activities of a program or phase, and transfer the completed product to others or close a cancelled program.

Control. Comparing actual performance with planned performance, analyzing variances, assessing trends to effect process improvements, evaluating possible alternatives, and recommending appropriate corrective action as needed.

Corporate Governance. The process by which an organization directs and controls its operational and strategic activities, and by which the organization responds to the legitimate rights, expectations, and desires of its stakeholders.

Customer. The person or organization that will use the program's benefits, products or services or result.

Executing Processes [Program Management Process Group]. Those processes performed to complete the work defined in the program management plan to accomplish the program's objectives defined in its scope statement.

Initiating Processes [Program Management Process Group]. Those processes performed to authorize and define the scope of a new phase or program, or that can result in the continuation of halted program work.

Input [Process Input]. Any item, whether internal or external to the program, that is required by a process before that process proceeds. May be an output from a predecessor process.

Mechanism. A means used to perform a process. (See also *Tool* or *Technique*.)

Monitoring and Controlling Processes [Program Management Process Group]. Those processes performed to measure and monitor program execution so that corrective action can be taken when necessary to control the execution of the phase or program.

Multi-Project Management. Those aspects of program management associated with initiating and coordinating the activities of multiple projects and the management of project managers.

Operational Management. Ongoing organizational activities associated with supporting functional elements, as opposed to project elements. Operational management also includes support of products that the organization has created through project activity.

Output. A product, result, or service generated by a process. May be an input to a successor process.

Performing Organization. The enterprise whose personnel are most directly involved in doing the work of the program.

Phase Gate. A review process at the end of a program phase where an oversight group, such as a program board or steering committee, decides to continue, continue with modification, or stop a program.

Planning Processes [Program Management Process Group]. Those processes performed to define and mature the program scope, develop the management plan, and identify and schedule the activities that occur within the program.

Process. A set of interrelated actions and activities performed to achieve a specified set of products, results, or services.

Program. A group of related projects managed in a coordinated way to obtain benefits and control not available from managing them individually. Programs may include elements of related work outside of the scope of the discrete projects in the program.

Program Governance. The process of developing, communicating, implementing, monitoring, and assuring the policies, procedures, organizational structures, and practices associated with a given program.

Program Management. The centralized coordinated management of a program to achieve the program's strategic objectives and benefits.

Program Management Process. Program management processes accomplish program management by receiving inputs and generating outputs, with the use of tools and techniques. In order to ensure that the outputs are delivered as required, the processes need to operate subject to controls.

Program Management Process Group. The process groups for program management comprise Initiating, Planning, Executing, Monitoring and Controlling, and Closing processes.

Program Stakeholders. Individuals and organizations that are actively involved in the program or whose interests may be positively or negatively affected by the program.

Project Management Process Group. A logical grouping of the project management processes described in the *PMBOK® Guide*. The project management process groups include Initiating Processes, Planning Processes, Executing Processes, Monitoring and Controlling Processes, and Closing Processes.

Sponsor. The person or group that provides the financial resources, in cash or in-kind, for the program.

Steering Committee. The group responsible for ensuring program goals are achieved and providing support to address program risks and issues. Sometimes this group is known as a Program Board or Governance Board.

Sustainment. Activities associated with ensuring that customers continue to receive utility from products.

Technique. A defined systematic procedure employed by a human resource to perform an activity to produce a product or result or deliver a service, and that may employ one or more tools.

Tool. Something tangible, such as a template or software program, used in performing an activity to produce a product or result.

Index by Keyword